TOWPE

The Kennet & Avon

Nick Corble

TEMPUS

First published 2006
Tempus Publishing Limited
The Mill, Brimscombe Port,
Stroud, Gloucestershire, GL5 2QG

British Library Cataloguing in Publication Data.
A catalogue record for this book is available from the British Library.

ISBN 0 7524 3763-1
Typesetting and design by Liz Rudderham
Origination by Tempus Publishing Limited
Printed and bound in Great Britain

CONTENTS

Bath
Claverton
Limpley Stoke
Winsley
Bradford -on-Avon
Semington
Seend
Devizes
Horton
All Cannings
Allington
Stanton St Bernard
Woodborough
Pewsey
Wilton
Great Bedwyn
Little Bedwyn
Hungerford
Kintbury
Newbury
Thatcham
Aldermaston
Theale
Reading

INTRODUCTION

The renaissance of the canals towards the latter end of the last century was one of the country's greatest, but largely unsung, success stories. A major new leisure resource emerged that somehow managed to bring together our collective love of the countryside, our pride in our past and our growing need for an escape from the fast pace of modern living. There is no doubt about it; the canals, once in danger of being filled in and erased from history, are here to stay.

Perhaps the most distinguishing feature of our canal system is the boats that ply their way slowly but steadily through it. However, although boaters clearly represent the most visible group of canal users, they are by no means the only ones to appreciate their worth. It has been estimated that over 400 million visits are made to the canal system each year, only 2 million of which are by boaters.

The reality is that the canals have become more than simply a transport system; they have evolved into visitor corridors. Walkers, riders, anglers, cyclists or simply those amongst the half of the population who live within 5 miles of an inland waterway, now regularly pass through these corridors. Cyclists alone account for three times as many visits as boaters and the total number expected to utilise the canals is expected to double over the coming decade.

These new Guides have been written to reflect this burgeoning reality. They will appeal to boaters but also to reach out beyond them to these other groups – the backpacker planning a towpath walk, motorists looking to spend a long weekend staying in bed and breakfasts, riders looking to discover the joy of towpath routes... the list goes on.

The Guides have been prepared to inform, amuse and spark an interest in the areas surrounding the canals, with the visitor corridor being defined as spanning 2 miles either side of the towpath. Anecdotes and interesting facts are scattered throughout the Guides to provide colour and bring these areas alive to the reader, with only the most resilient likely to resist the temptation to repeat at least some of these to their companions.

For ease of use, each canal is broken down into sections covering between 7–13 miles, with sections themselves broken down into the following four groupings:

SHAPERS
Describing the route of the canal, the local history associated with it and details of the natural landscape and transport links, this section provides the basic background to each section.

BASICS

Where to shop, find a pub or locate a place to stay as well as places to eat, all these topics are covered under this heading, taking the sting out of finding your way around and the essentials of getting by.

SEEING AND DOING

What to look out for and where it's worth making a diversion to see that oddity or curiosity you might not otherwise find, plus where to find that something a bit special culturally or where to go if you simply want to be entertained.

SAMPLING

Ways to dip into the local area and become part of the landscape, whether you are walking or cycling (a recommended route is provided for both in each section), riding, fishing or want to wander around a golf course.

Each section is accompanied by maps complete with symbols to show you where to find places highlighted in the text, with larger symbols indicating a concentration of pubs, hotels etc. Phone numbers and websites are given as appropriate and the 'Learn More and Links' section provides pointers on where to look if you want to follow up on items covered in the Guide – making it simple if you want to check a pub's opening hours, whether a Leisure Centre has a squash court or the times of a local bus.

We hope that these new Guides will encourage more people to enjoy our inland waterways and help them to deepen their appreciation of the symbiotic relationship between the canals and the towns and villages that surround them.

Nick Corble
Series Editor

NOTE: Cyclists need a permit from British Waterways – either apply direct or download one from their website www.britishwaterways.co.uk. Likewise, anglers should check who controls fishing rights on particular stretches and details are provided in the sampling section.

OVERVIEW

The Kennet & Avon Canal is a modern success story, a tale of how a determined band of volunteers came together to rescue and restore part of the nation's heritage and create a new leisure resource. Years of campaigning and sheer hard work culminated in 1990 with the re-opening of the canal by the Queen, thus ending forty years when the route existed only in parts.

Fittingly, this act took place at what remains perhaps as the canal's most impressive feature and main stumbling block to restoration: the Caen Hill flight of locks outside Devizes. This was fitting, because it had been the completion of the Caen Hill flight that marked the initial completion of the canal 180 years before. This dramatic feature sits at the western end of the canal's long summit that winds through the picturesque Vale of Pewsey and marks the beginning of the route through the counties of Wiltshire and Avon that ends with further drama with the drop into the heart of Bath.

The Kennet & Avon is historically seen as three waterways: the Kennet Navigation from Newbury to Reading, opened in 1723; the Avon Navigation from Bristol to Bath opened in 1727; and a manmade middle section linking Bath with Newbury opened in 1810. Given the quite different nature of the Avon Navigation, which is largely tidal, this Guide concentrates on the route from Reading to Bath only. The section between Bristol and Bath had, in fact, been navigable as early as the thirteenth century, but the mills also attracted to the waters soon made it impossible for boats to make the journey.

The dream of a route linking Bristol and the nation's capital came alive during the eighteenth and early nineteenth centuries through a combination of geographical and political factors. Not only did Atlantic storms along the southern part of the country make the coastal route a hazardous proposition but regular spats with the French also made shipping vulnerable to attack.

As the Industrial Revolution kicked in, the need to transport bulky goods inland between the Severn and the Thames became more pressing and plans were drawn up. Commencement was delayed, however, by bureaucratic hold ups. An initial meeting had been held in Hungerford in April 1788, chaired by Charles Dundas, the MP for Berkshire, which led to the formation of a committee which agreed to survey what was at that time called The Western Canal.

Although a survey took place a second was subsequently commissioned in 1791, this time from the engineer John Rennie. Although he agreed with the broad conclusions of the first survey, that an adequate supply of water was available, it was agreed at this point that construction would not commence until £75,000 had been raised, further delaying the start.

Little Bedwyn Lock.

Two years later the committee had singularly failed in this task and, by now exasperated by the lack of progress, a group of Bristol business-men began to plot to take the project over. In one evening alone these men raised over £250,000 in share subscriptions and Charles Dundas had to move quickly to accommodate this new group.

Yet another survey, again by Rennie, led to a shift in the originally proposed route, missing out Marlborough and taking in Devizes instead, much to the chagrin of the burghers of the former who had to be smoothed over with the offer of reduced road tolls between the two towns.

A fourth survey resulted in the summit being pushed further north, avoiding the need for a 2-mile-long tunnel through the creation of the Crofton Locks and pumping station, a move which saved over £40,000. Another shorter tunnel did have to be built, however, when a local landowner, Lord Bruce, refused to countenance a deep cutting through his land, leading to the construction of a 502-yard tunnel that still bears his name.

Work was finally completed over thirty years after the initial commit-tee meeting, thirty years the canal could not afford to lose as it was not long afterwards that the railways came. In a sign of the way things were going, it took less than quarter of a century before a proposal emerged to convert the canal into a railway by rough walling its sides. Although this was defeated, it was a matter of time before the canal met the fate of so many other waterways and was bought by its tracked rival, in this case the Great Western Railway (GWR).

The GWR had duplicated the route of the canal, as is all too evident to towpath travellers today, and their intentions in buying the canal were certainly not honourable. Maintenance suffered and the familiar story of decline followed, so that by the early years of the twentieth century the canal was almost impossible to navigate in places. By the 1930s regular traffic had disappeared and by the late 1940s through passage was rare.

A Canal Trust was formed fairly soon after the war, but again, initial progress was slow. As late as the 1980s the Caen Hill flight was a relic, although when change came it came quickly, and by the end of that decade restoration was complete. Today the canal is regarded by many as one of the most beautiful on the system, offering a variety of landscapes, a range of towns to visit, long stretches of open water and a fair amount of challenge.

Indeed, boaters who find gentle cruising with barely a lock or obstacle to negotiate too boring will find this is the canal for them. The early stages in particular are crowded with a procession of swing and lift bridges as well as locks that, although functioning, are clearly in need of some tender loving care. Some of the lock gates leak so badly they look as if they have been peppered by gunfire. Each bridge is different with many requiring not only stopping your boat but also the local traffic, offering the opportunity to play policeman.

But for walkers and cyclists the route is much more relaxing, with the towpath generally in very good condition throughout. Furthermore, things get better after Newbury and there is a long lock-free stretch along the summit between Crofton and Devizes as the canal winds its way along and through the Vale of Pewsey – the so-called Long Pound, which provides a welcome respite before the challenge of Caen Hill.

This is a highly accessible canal, with both the railway and A4 making most of it readily available so that it can be sampled in stages. It can also be a tricky one to navigate, with the rivers that make up a lot of its routes demanding respect. Warning signs and weirs are a common feature at the Kennet end of the canal and currents can at times be powerful enough to require a strong arm at the tiller.

Generally, however, although this is a waterway that requires some investment of effort, at least for boaters, this effort is amply rewarded. This Guide allows the towpath traveller to access the delights the Kennet & Avon offers, many of which are just off the towpath itself and as such are easily missed.

The Guide starts at the Reading end, a large city with every conceivable amenity, as is Bath at the western end. In between, towns such as Newbury, Hungerford, Pewsey, Devizes, Trowbridge and Bradford on Avon sit on or near the canal, offering opportunities to stock up on supplies and get in touch with 'civilisation'. Alternatively, there is an equal supply of smaller villages such as Kintbury, Great Bedwyn, Wootton Rivers and All Cannings, all of which offer as a minimum a pub and often more.

The abiding memory of this canal is less of towns and more of wide open stretches lined with nothing but fields and the possibility of not

Honey Street Bridge with the Alton Barnes white horse in the distance.

meeting another soul all day. The stretch between Hungerford and Devizes, taking in the Crofton Flight and the Long Pound, is a particular favourite for many, as is the meandering approach to Bath after the two aqueducts of Avoncliff and Dundas, west of Bradford on Avon.

Rivers are a constant companion, starting with the Kennet and following with the Dun and then the Avon, and the origins of much of the canal as a 'canalised' river are at times all too evident, with long, straight stretches a particular feature. Generally this works to the canal's advantage, with broad steep-sided valleys and an abundant variety of wildlife. At times, such as the lead in to Bath, this means some dramatic views, in this instance over the Avon Valley.

As has already been suggested, the Kennet & Avon is a success story, and it is a story which is not yet over. Recent investment is set to continue and, with the future now secured, the canal deserves to be visited, sampled and enjoyed by all types of towpath user, be they boater, walker, cyclist or fisherman. We hope this Guide will act as a useful introduction for those new to the canal and reveal fresh insights for those to whom it is an old friend.

SECTION A

READING TO ALDERMASTON WHARF

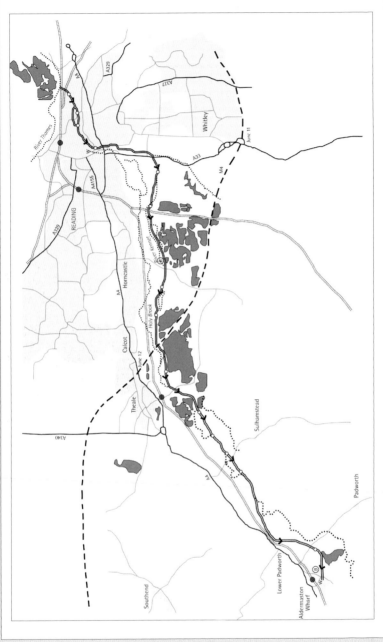

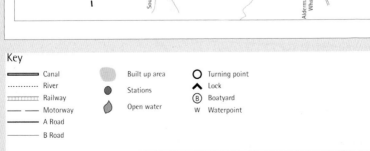

Key

▬▬▬	Canal		Built up area	○	Turning point	
··········	River		Stations	▲	Lock	
▥▥▥▥	Railway		Open water	Ⓑ	Boatyard	
– – –	Motorway			W	Waterpoint	
▬▬▬	A Road					
▬▬▬	B Road					

Reading
Whitley
Horncastle
Calcot
Theale
Sulhamstead
Padworth
Southend
Lower Padworth
Aldermaston Wharf

River Thames
Holy Brook
June 11
June 12

A329
A4
A4155
A33
A327
A340
M4

SHAPERS

THE CANAL ON THIS STRETCH

KEY FACTS

LENGTH: 10 miles

BOATYARDS: 2

Kennet Cruises, Early
Reading Marine, Aldermaston

WATERPOINTS: 3

County Lock
Tyle Mill
Aldermaston

TURNING POINTS: 14

Blake's Lock	Calcot
Abbey Loop (North)	Garston Lock
Abbey Loop (South)	Sulhamstead Lock
County Lock	Sulhamstead Weir
Fobney Lock	Tyle Mill
Milkmaid's Footbridge	Ufton Swing Bridge
Burghfield Lock	Padworth Lock

NB: There are numerous 'unofficial' opportunities to turn along this stretch, although boaters should always be wary of currents.

LOCKS: 11

Blake's Lock (3ft 6in)	Sheffield Lock (2ft 2in)
County Lock (1ft 2in)	Sulhamstead Lock (4ft 1in)
Fobney Lock (7ft8in)	Tyle Mill Lock (6ft 4in)
Southcot Lock (5ft 3in)	Towney Lock (9ft 8in)
Burghfield Lock (7ft)	Padworth Lock (5ft 1in)
Garston Lock (7ft 7in)	

After the Thames the canal adopts the River Kennet, a fact that should not be forgotten as currents can be an issue along here. After the not altogether unpleasant urban landscape of Reading the vista opens up and the pattern of long 'canalised' stretches of waterway, interspersed with the locks and swing bridges that are to become a hallmark of the canal, soon begin.

The initial approach to the canal from the Thames is unpromising, the opening itself sitting at the end of a long line

Blake's Lock is the only non-Thames lock managed by the Thames Conservancy.

of moorings favoured by boaters as they provide access to a local Tesco. Gas storage tanks line one bank. with pipelines and the railway soon passing over the water. Almost immediately there is a turning point for those unwilling or unable to negotiate Blake's Lock.

The waterway is now firmly in Reading, and boaters looking to stop for a while should use the Abbey Loop to the right. Moorings are available either side of a bridge, although safety in numbers is better guaranteed on the far side, under the shadow of Reading Abbey and Gaol. Reading is a good example of a town that has taken the river to its heart; indeed, it has become a distinguishing feature of the

> Passage through the Oracle complex is controlled by traffic lights and care needs to be taken with the unpredictable current at this point, but for walkers ignorant of the stresses faced by passing boaters this is a pleasant stroll.

new Oracle shopping and entertainment complex, where, if the sun is out, an almost Mediterranean-style café society prevails.

Officially, the towpath runs along the left bank through modern housing and office development, but in practice it is possible to pass by on the right as well for most of this stretch, and boats can be turned at either end of the Abbey Loop. The controlled section ends at the shallow County Lock to the left, where the windlass has to be retrieved as from now on boaters are on their own; the Kennet & Avon is best served with an unconventional $1^1/_8$in gauge, although a normal 1in or $1^1/_4$in will do.

The towpath moves over to the right as the river takes on more of a canal-like appearance after some moored boats. Road and pipe bridges cross over the water and town houses and commercial premises line the banks, along with an unconscionable number of sunken dinghies!

The luxury of just over a mile of lock-free canal ends at Fobney Lock, where the scenery becomes more rural as the towpath switches to the left and becomes generally more solid. Again, the current can also be significant here. After the lock there is a long straight to a railway bridge and then Southcot Lock after the charmingly named Milkmaid's Bridge, just before which there is another turning point. Boaters need to be aware, however, that the bridge is not the one straight ahead, but another hidden away to the right.

These long straights are characteristic of the canal along here and represent fresh cuts made where the river could not be made navigable. Meadowland stretches to the right, whilst trees hide the view on the other side. Towards the end of this straight there is a long line of boats on long-term permits, and members of the Burghfield Island Boat Club (01256 320968). The thatched Cunning Man pub follows Burghfield Bridge and the towpath slopes over to the right shortly after the wooden Swan's Bridge, where there is a turning point, which in turn precedes Burghfield Lock.

A pleasant wooded section follows with the towpath threading through the side of a meadow with the railway getting ever closer from the right. The largely hidden flooded gravel pits begin on the left although the towpath crosses once again at the pretty Hissey's Bridge and allows the occasional glimpse of the water below.

The M4 breaks the tranquillity briefly but is soon a forgotten interruption in the run up to Garston Lock, one of two turf-sided locks on this stretch. Bereft of solid sides, these need to be left empty after use so as not to drown and undermine the fragile natural banks. Shallow water and vibrant bank-side growth argue against mooring along here, but they do contribute towards a good variety of wildlife.

Just after the modest Sheffield Lock there is the double attraction of the first electric swing bridge (Theale) and the first set of 48-hour visitors' moorings. A BW key grants the boater the opportunity to hold up the traffic in order to pass his boat through, although this is by no means the last such occasion where he can exercise this power.

> Boaters should be aware that Aldermaston Lift Bridge just before the lock does not operate during rush hour (4.30-5.45 p.m.).

The gravel pits now become a close companion as the canal enters another twisty section prior to Sulhamstead Lock.

There is more long-term mooring after the swing bridge and a lock at Tyle Mill (where there is a waterpoint), although the bank has been reinforced with environmentally friendly woven branches. After Ufton Swing Bridge the railway, always close, comes right alongside the towpath, again not for the last time. Townley Lock can be vicious and Padworth Swing Bridge shortly after can be confusing as it will not operate until the heavy road barriers have been manipulated manually.

If all this is proving too much for boaters there is an opportunity to turn just before Padworth Lock, and a small visitors' centre run by the Kennet & Avon Trust lies between this and Aldermaston Lock, as does the long approach to the Reading Marine Co., a favourite for hirers.

PRINCIPAL TOWNS AND VILLAGES ALONG THIS STRETCH

ALDERMASTON WHARF
Distinct from the village that also bears its name, Aldermaston Wharf is defined by its canal visitors' centre and boatyard, although a lift bridge over the canal and railway station also lend it significance.

> Aldermaston Wharf was the site of a Roman villa, but only its bathhouse remains.

CALCOT
A district of Reading with semi-detached housing and bungalows predominant and more recent estates.

HORNCASTLE
Another district of Reading populated mainly with low-rise flats.

LOWER PADWORTH
A few small bungalows strung out along the A4 with a large hotel.

PADWORTH
Padworth College and church are pretty much all that remain of Padworth, but the latter is worth a visit.

READING
A modern-looking town with an ancient past, Reading has become the regional capital of the Thames Valley and acts as a focal point for local services and transport networks. Despite initial appearances, it is worth scratching away at the town's surface, beneath which a distinguished history lies.

SOUTHEND
A linear village now more or less part of nearby Bradfield with an impressive war memorial on its northern edge.

SULHAMSTEAD
A scattered village distinguished mainly by the fact that it plays host to the Thames Valley Police Training College, which can be seen from the A4.

THEALE
Sitting just off the A4, the motorway has provided a barrier to prevent Theale being swallowed up by Reading, and it retains a clear distinct identity, with a small town feel.

WHITLEY
Helped by a ridge of high ground to the east and north and the Kennet to the west, Whitley is a suburb of Reading that just about hangs on to its own identity.

> Whitley was once known for its 'Whitley Whiff', caused by the (thankfully now closed) nearby sewage works.

HISTORY

Reading acts as the eastern limit of the Kennet & Avon Canal, with the canal and the first river in its name providing a convenient southern boundary to the town. To the north much the same job is done by the Thames, and given these natural advantages it is no surprise that this spot has proved popular with settlers through the centuries.

Reading's influence dominates this section, a position it has enjoyed for at least the last 2,000 years. The town's name is thought to derive from the Celtic word *Rhydd*, meaning ford, although the crossing in question would have been over the Kennet rather than the Thames.

Although these days Reading gives off a very modern appearance, you don't have to scratch too hard to reveal a place where kings and queens, archbishops and friars, parliamentarians and royalists have helped to shape both local and national history. They have done so using means as diverse as battles, sieges, weddings and murders, with much of the evidence of this activity remaining today.

Man settled here early, with plenty to suggest that there used to be an Iron Age hill fort in the very centre of the modern town, in the Northumberland Avenue area. The Romans also had a village to the south. Ancient earthworks around Padworth have been attributed to the Roman period, or its immediate aftermath, describing the northern limits of the Roman town of Silchester. These ditches are thought to have been dug by followers of a king who established himself as a local protector just after the Romans left.

It was the Saxons, though, who began to settle in the surrounding area in earnest. An alternative view on the origin of Reading's name is that it derives from a local Saxon leader known as Reada. Part of the attraction was the waterways, with riverside settlements well placed for trading.

> The Saxons called the ditches around Padworth 'Grim's Ditch' as they assumed that they must have been built by a God such as Woden, who was also known as Grim.

Reading was briefly a Viking headquarters following their invasion of Britain in 860, although little evidence remains of their stay. They were 'persuaded' to leave by King Alfred of Wessex, his kingdom being one of the greatest in the land, although it frequently came up against that of Mercia, with modern Berkshire a regular battleground. The area covered in this section therefore remained Saxon rather than being incorporated into the Danelaw.

It was around this time that many of the towns and villages covered here became established, including Kintbury, Thatcham, Padworth and Aldermaston. The last of these initially vied with Reading for influence, being a base for the king's local representative, responsible for most of modern-day Berkshire.

> Queen Aelfthrith's face, along with that of four of her nuns, features on Reading's shield.

This individual was known as the Ealdorman, with Ealdorman's Town being the origin of the modern-day place name. Aldermaston was, in effect, his country retreat, with most of his time spent at Wallingford. Slowly, Reading began to gain the promi-

> It was at Reading Abbey in 1185 that the Patriarch of Jerusalem offered Henry II the crown to his city if he would defend it against the infidels, an offer Henry had the wisdom to turn down.

nence we see today. Signs of its growing importance include the establishment of a royal nunnery there in 979 by Queen Aelfthrith, who wished to atone for the dreadful act of murdering her stepson St Edward in order to make her own son, Ethelred, king.

Around the time of the conquest this part of Berkshire was thriving, with Reading alone having six mills and the road linking London and Bath (the modern A4) proving to be a valuable trading route. Shortly afterwards, Reading also became a place of pilgrimage, with the foundation of its Abbey by Henry I in 1121.

Originally a family mausoleum, the Abbey was built on the former Viking site and became a wealthy monastery. It was also, very briefly, home to a motte and bailey castle, constructed during the civil war between Henry's daughter the Empress Matilda and King Stephen, the remains of which can be seen in Forbury Gardens.

The Abbey grew in importance and during times of plague Parliament would retreat westwards to meet there, with the Commons gathering in the Chapter House and the Lords in

> Not all of Henry I was buried at the Abbey; Rouen in France took possession of his bowels, brains, heart, eyes and tongue.

the Refectory. The Abbey also witnessed a number of weddings, including that of Edward IV in 1464. Kings, queens and princes were also buried here, such was its importance, including Henry I and his daughter Empress Maud of the Holy Roman Empire.

Meanwhile, villages in the surrounding area benefited from being in Reading's shadow, and to a lesser extent to being near to the Royal Court at Windsor. Families strip-farmed the local land growing crops of wheat, oats, barley, rye and beans.

As elsewhere, the Black Death had a devastating effect, not least because it combined with a period of poor harvests and disease amongst the sheep. As the rural hinterland recovered it found the basis of fresh economic prosperity in corn, utilising the available trading routes to sell crops in London.

With the Tudors Reading retained its prominence, and wool once again became important to the local economy, with sheep prospering on the Berkshire Downs. Reading and Thatcham, in particular, became known for their production of clothing yarns, a reputation the area hung onto for many centuries. This period marked the end of the Abbey, though, as Henry VIII dissolved the monasteries. The abbot at the time, despite being a great friend of Henry, was hanged for the offence of trying to save his Abbey.

In Elizabeth's time, Reading's Guild built their own Guild Hall, a sign of their growing prosperity. The increasing importance of wool also meant enclosures, and these were tough times for those living off the land as local noblemen established themselves and built their manor houses off the backs of the profits made from their villagers' land.

> The Abbey was home to 234 religious relics, including the head of St Philip and the hand of St James. The latter was discovered bricked up at Reading and can now be seen in Marlow Roman Catholic Church (Bucks).

> The Oracle shopping centre that now dominates the centre of town shares its name and site with a workhouse for poor clothiers set up in 1643.

The Civil War also left its mark. Declaring at first for Parliament, it changed its mind and welcomed the Royalist army, with the town becoming the king's second largest stronghold after Oxford. Feeding the king's 3,000 troops practically bankrupted the town and eventually the Earl of Essex laid siege, the town falling after ten days. Skirmishes also took place at Theale and Padworth, the latter resulting in the massacre of 300 Parliamentarians.

Further fighting followed during the Glorious Revolution of 1688 in the Battle of Broad Street. This, the only battle of the so-called revolution, took place when William of Orange's army met the Irish troops of James and roundly defeated them.

> Where W.H. Smith now stands was the birthplace in the early seventeenth century of William Laud, who became the Archbishop of Canterbury.

> Within twenty years of its foundation, Huntley & Palmers had the largest biscuit factory in the world.

In more peaceful times, the area continued to exploit the munificence of its geology and geography and embraced the industrial age. In the nineteenth century Reading became known for its '3 Bs', of brewing (in modern times the Courage brewery), bulbs (Reading was home to Sutton Seeds) and biscuits. A certain Joseph Huntley moved into 72 London Street in 1811 and baked biscuits for those using the Crown coaching inn opposite. He was joined thirty years later by George Palmer, a local benefactor, and Huntley & Palmers was born.

Not all was straightforward, however, with changes in agriculture not always welcomed. The Kintbury Riots of 1830 led to ringleaders being transported to Australia, one of a number of 'swing riots' involving the destruction of new farm machinery.

> In Victorian times Reading was known for its Reading sauce. Said to be like Worcester sauce, it was for a long time more popular.

Industrial progress was also welcomed and Reading became one of the country's first railway towns. Lines proliferated, impacting badly on the finances of both the canals and the traditional coaching routes. Meanwhile, traditional arable farming gave way to dairy.

Reading continued to grow at the expense of surrounding villages, with some of these in time absorbed into 'greater Reading'. Some found a niche, such as Aldermaston with its nuclear weapons centre and others as high-tech computer centres, but mostly they found a new role as dormitory settlements to Reading which retains the role it has held for centuries of being a major regional centre.

THE NATURAL LANDSCAPE

The landscape in this section is defined by water, with the stately Thames to the north and the more exuberant Kennet to the south along with a series of lakes (mostly old gravel pits) to the south of the Kennet. As this might imply, gradients are slight, although Reading itself sits slightly higher than the two floodplains to its north and south. The landscape rises slightly to the west around Southend, with a series of small woods and copses leavening the otherwise flat and fairly featureless scenery.

ACCESS AND TRANSPORT

ROADS
As this section begins the A329 provides a boundary to the north, whilst the M4 does the same job in the south. Meanwhile, the A4 follows the sweep of the canal to the north, eventually coming alongside it at Aldermaston, passing through Theale along the way. With two junctions on the motorway (Junctions 11 and 12) access to the area is relatively easy.

The A4 is in fact a fairly constant companion to the canal in its early stages, with a number of minor roads leading off it. In addition, the A33 leads north from Junction 11 into the heart of Reading while the A327 passes through the south of the city. Once in Aldermaston, the A340 (the Basingstoke Road) takes the visitor south. Due to the succession of reservoirs in the canal's early stages, along with the presence of the River Kennet, access to the towpath itself is best achieved from the north in this section.

RAIL
There are four railway stations along this section: Reading, Reading West, Theale and Aldermaston. Reading is a busy junction offering both intercity and local services as well as bus links. Theale and Aldermaston are both on the company's Kennet Line, as is Reading West, although this sits on a spur heading down to the south coast.

> When it was opened in 1840 Reading was the temporary western terminus for the GWR. The effect was dramatic, being faster that the nearest alternative (the stagecoach) by a quarter. The following year the line was extended to Bristol, but Reading has remained a major interchange.

First Great Western (08457 484950) also operate a North Downs Line out of Reading heading to Gatwick via Guildford, a Thames Valley & West London Line into London Paddington, a Cotswold Line linking Paddington with Hereford and finally the Oxford & Thames Valley Line heading up to Leamington Spa via Oxford and Banbury.

Virgin Trains (0870 7891234) also operate cross-country trains running through Reading, notably linking Birmingham and the south coast, whilst South West Trains (0845 6000650) operates a suburban line linking the town with London Waterloo.

For more detailed information contact National Train Enquiries on 08457 484950 or www.nationalrail.co.uk.

BUSES

The following list sets out the main bus services on this section although it is advisable to check before using them as some buses only run on certain days and others may have been withdrawn since publication of this Guide. It is also worth checking for more local services, in particular those linking districts of Reading, where there are a number of circular and school term-time only services.

- 44/45 – *regular Calcot to Reading service (Reading Buses)*
- 73 – *links Aldermaston and Reading via Padworth Common and Sulhamstead on Wednesdays only (Four Valleys)*
- 101 – *Newbury to Reading via Theale (Reading Buses)*
- 102 – *Reading to Newbury via Calcot, Theale and Woolhampton (Reading Buses)*
- 104/5 – *Newbury to Calcot via Aldermaston and Theale (Reading Buses)*
- 148 – *Reading to Tadley via Padworth (Reading Buses)*
- N4/N5 – *circular via Whitley Wood, evenings only (Reading Buses)*
- N7 – *Reading to Calcot, evenings only (Reading Buses)*

In addition to the above, there are regular services linking Reading Station with both Heathrow and Gatwick airports.

Contact details for bus operators in this area are listed below, although Traveline (www.traveline.org.uk) on 0870 6082608 can give details of specific services between 7 a.m. and 10 p.m.:
- Four Valleys Minibus Services, Newbury (01635 35806)
- Reading Buses, Reading (01189 594000)

TAXIS

The following list gives a selection of the taxi operators in this section:

- 1st Yellow Cars, Reading (01189 660666)
- Abbey Cars, Reading (01189 454545)
- Alexander Taxis, Reading (01189 882979)
- Candy Cars, Theale (01189 304179)
- Falcon Cars, Reading (01189 561111)
- Global Cars, Reading (01189 666888)
- Miracle Taxis, Reading (01189 500500)
- Reading Cars, Reading (01189 594949)
- Thames Valley Taxis, Reading (01189 484848)
- Theale Taxis, Theale (01189 302345)

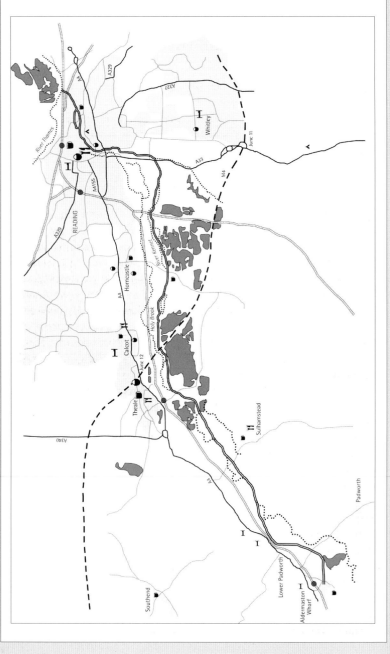

Key

▬▬▬	Canal		Built up area	◗	Shops	● Pub
·········	River	●	Stations		Accomodation	⋔ Restaurant
⊞⊞⊞⊞	Railway	◖	Open water	H	Accomodation	
▬ ▬ ▬	Motorway			⋏	Campsite	
▬▬▬	A Road					
▬▬▬	B Road					

BASICS

INTRODUCTION

Reading offers a comprehensive base for meeting basic needs at the very start of the canal. Other centres such as Theale and Aldermaston should not be discounted, however, and it should come as no surprise that there are a number of good pubs strung out along the old coaching route of the A4.

SHOPPING

Reading dominates shopping in this section, in particular its modernistic Oracle Centre opened in 1999. As well as all the usual High Street names this has two department stores, House of Fraser and Debenhams. A particular feature of the Oracle is the River Kennet, which flows through its centre, providing an opportunity for Continental-style waterside relaxation, but with a British twist in that most of the outlets are part of a chain and run by dour youths rather than enthusiastic families.

In March 2001 Reading's Oracle Centre was voted 'Best New Large Shopping Centre in Europe' by no less an authority than the International Council of Shopping Centres.

Reading also has the recently refurbished Broad Street Mall, which has a John Lewis and Marks & Spencer, and an extensive paved High Street. A Farmer's Market is held on the first and third Saturday morning of every month at the Old Cattle Market in Reading.

Shops also line the A4 out of Reading, but these are mainly local in nature, with a newsagent at Calcot and an Aldi supermarket as well as a mini-market at Horncastle, along with a Tesco Express. Just before the road reaches the motorway there is an out-of-town centre with a large Sainsbury's, a Boots, Next and Sports World.

Theale has a pleasantly paved High Street which encourages traffic to slow to walking pace and is convenient if you do not want to go into Reading. There is a Co-op supermarket and post office as well as a range of other basic shops including a pizza and sandwich bar, an off-licence, newsagent and a Lloyds Bank. There is also a shop selling sculptor's tools and materials should inspiration overcome you.

Shops also line the A4 and there is a post office and stores at Cold Ash.

EATING AND DRINKING

Reading is again the focus for eating and drinking in this section. The town is well served with pubs, and visitors are advised to try their luck, with the following representing only a sample of what is available:

- The Allied Arms
  (01189 590865)
- The Blagrave Arms
  (01189 571194)
- The Brewery Tap
  (01189 576280)
- The Eldon Arms
  (01189 713202)
- The Jolly Anglers
  (01189 261666)
- The Honey Pot (01189 566870)

- The Hook and Tackle
  (01189 500830)
- The Hope Tap
  (01189 582266)
- The Pitcher and Piano
  (01189 588964)
- The Purple Turtle
  (01189 597196)
- The Rising Sun (01189 572974)
- The Slug and Lettuce
  (01189 571839)

Other pubs in the section include:

- The Cunning Man, Burghfield
  (01189 590771) – *canalside*
- The Horncastle, Horncastle
  (01189 451265)
- The Sun Inn, Whitchurch Hill,
  Reading (01189 842260)
- The Bull, Theale (01189
  303478)
- The Crown Inn, Theale
  (01189 302310)
- The Falcon, Theale
  (01189 302523)
- The Fox and Hounds, Theale
  (01189 302295)

- The Lamb, Theale
  (01189 302357)
- Red Lion, Theale
  (01189 302394)
- The Thatchers Arms, Theale
  (01189 302070)
- The Volunteer, Theale
  (01189 302489)
- The Spring Inn, Sulhamstead
  (01189 302307)
- The Queens Head, Southend
  (01189 744332)
- The Butt Inn, Aldermaston
  Wharf (01189 712129)

When it comes to eating the Riverside complex in the Oracle Centre has eighteen restaurants and cafés, including the following, as well as a number of pubs:

- Bar 38 (01189 566832)
- Bar Med (01189 519990)
- Chilis Grill and Bar
  (01189 574787)
- Ma Potters Chargrill
  (01189 566963)

- Nandos Chickenland
  (01189 502199)
- Old Orleans (01189 512678)
- Yellow River
  (01189 567009)

The Broad Street Mall also has a selection of smaller cafés and fast-food outlets. Otherwise, the following list provides a selection of places to eat in the town:

- China Palace, Oxford Road
  (01189 572323) – *Chinese*
- Crostini, Kings Road

  (01189 571362) – *Mediterranean*
- Dhaka Spice, Queen's Walk
  (01189 391012) – *Indian*

- Hong Kong Fish Bar, Oxford Road (01189 507303) – *fish and chips*
- Mali Thai, Queens Walk (01189 596670) – *Thai*
- Pepe Sale, Queens Walk (01189 597700) – *Sardinian*
- Standard Nepalese Tandoori, Caversham Road (01189 590093) – *Nepalese/Indian*
- Sweeney and Todd, Castle Street (01189 586466) – *pies*
- Topo Gigio, Kings Walk (01189 500070) – *Italian*

Restaurants outside of Reading include:

- Murdoch's Restaurant, Calcot (01189 451344) – *British*
- Café Blue Cobra, Theale (01189 304040) – *Thai*
- Hussey's Takeaway and Bakery, Theale (01189 302764)
- King Wok, Theale
- (01189 303921) – *Chinese*
- Silsila Tandoori, Calcot (01189 417551)
- The Spring Inn, Sulhamstead (01189 302307) – *à la carte pub dining*

Finally, the Kennet & Avon Canal Trust has a small café at its centre on Aldermaston Wharf (01189 712868).

SLEEPING

There is a good selection of hotels, both in and around Reading and elsewhere, ranging from the modest to large international chains and conference centres.

HOTELS

- Abbey House Hotel, Reading (01189 590549) – *budget hotel*
- The Bath Hotel, Reading (01189 572019) – *twenty-three rooms*
- Beech House Hotel, Reading (01189 591901) – *fifteen rooms, Victorian house*
- Comfort Inn, Reading (01189 311311) – *large Victorian building*
- Holiday Inn, Reading South (0870 4009067)
- The Lawn and Parkside Hotels, Reading (01189 590342)
- Renaissance Hotel, Queens Walk, Reading (01189 586222)
- Royal County Hotel, Duke
- Street, Reading (01189 583455)
- Travelodge, Whitley (0870 1911708)
- Holiday Inn, Whitley (01189 259988)
- The Calcot Hotel, Calcot (01189 416423)
- Pincents Manor Hotel, Calcot (01189 323511)
- The Old Lamb, Theale (01189 302357)
- Comfort Inn, Reading South, Lower Padworth (01189 713282)
- Marriot Courtyard Hotel, Lower Padworth (01189 714411)
- The Manor House Hotel, Aldermaston (01189 819333)

BED AND BREAKFAST/GUEST HOUSES

- Abadair House, Reading (01189 863792)
- Carriacou Lodge, Reading (01189 752872)
- Roses B&B, Reading (01189 313394)
- The Avenue Guest House, Reading (01189 313394)

- Arch Guest House, Reading (01189 872221)
- Fairview Guest House, Reading (01189 391955)
- The Reading Hotel, Reading (01189 872076)
- Hinds Head, Aldermaston (01189 712194)

CAMPING

Camping is possible along this stretch at:
- Loddon Court Farm, Reading (01189 883153) – *residential caravans*
- Sunnylands, Reading (01734 833707)
- Wellington Country Park, Reading (01189 326444) – *pitches for tents, caravans and motor caravans within 350-acre country park*

The nearest camping supplies outlets in this section are:
- Altinus, Broad Street Mall, Reading (01189 582211)
- Blacks, St Mary's Butts, Reading (01189 595150)
- Cotswold Outdoor, Basingstoke Road, Reading (01189 875177)
- Millets, St Mary's Butts, Reading (01189 595228)
- Millets, Friars Walk, Reading (01189 569506)

The Salmon Run, Walk A.

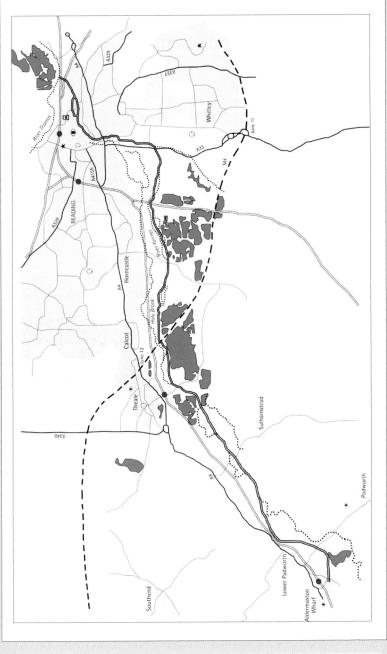

Key

━━━	Canal		●	Site/Sight
⋯⋯	River	Built up area	◎	Leisure
▦▦▦	Railway	Stations	★	Entertainment
━ ━	Motorway	Open water	♛	Culture
━━	A Road			
──	B Road			

SEEING AND DOING

INTRODUCTION

G iven its long and distinguished history, it should come as no surprise that Reading has much to offer the casual visitor. Perhaps it is the uncompromising modernity of much of the recent building that makes it so? The guiding hand of the local authority can be felt on many of the local attractions, but this is a benign force and one that generally works to the attractions' advantage.

> 'Few towns are less prepossessing at first glance than Reading... but few towns better repay exploration' – Sir John Betjeman.

Reading has a Tourist Information Centre based in Church House (01189 566226).

SIGHTS

T he Town Hall complex in the centre of the town, which includes the Museum of Reading, is a good example of Reading's determination to be taken seriously. Opened during 1872–75, this is a complex of three buildings which also includes the concert hall. The

> Kennet Cruises, based in Earley in Reading (0118 987 1115), offers public trips on the *Lancing* and also has a day-hire boat, *Rosina Emma*.

Town Hall was designed by local man Alfred Waterhouse and is hard to miss, being constructed in the High Gothic style.

The museum (01189 399800) is designed to be 'family friendly' and traces the history of Reading and the surrounding area, taking the visitor back to the Saxon era and right through the town's Victorian heyday and current role as a 'magnet' town for large firms within the Thames Valley. A highlight of the museum is a replica of the Bayeaux Tapestry and another is the Silchester Gallery, where it is possible to see a range of Roman goods discovered at the nearby site of Calleva Atrebatum.

Reading is, in fact, blessed with a variety of museums including the museum of English Rural Life on Redlands Road (01189 318660), which houses a fascinating collection and looks at farmers and farming over the last 150 years. The University of Reading on Shinfield Road also offers two museums, the Ure Museum of Greek Archaeology (01189 318420), the fourth largest collection of Greek ceramics in the country, and the Cole Museum of Zoology (01189 318903), 4,000 specimens housed in the foyer of the School of Animal and Microbial Science.

To many, the name of Reading will always be associated with its famous and still somewhat formidable gaol, which sits alongside the Abbey Loop in the centre of town. This was designed in the 1830s as a model prison and its most famous prisoner was Oscar Wilde, who was sent there due to concerns for his health during his incarceration for 'moral offences'. His cell survives, but cannot be visited. Wilde aficionados can, however, enjoy extracts of his work in an homage of artwork by the artist Bruce Robinson, outside the gaol on the waterfront along Chestnut Walk. In what can be seen as something of a come-down, or perhaps a sign of the times, these days the gaol is a Youth Offenders' Centre.

> A common misconception is that *The Ballad of Reading Gaol* was written by Wilde during his incarceration in the town. In fact, it was written afterwards during his exile in France and tells of the feelings of a prisoner towards a fellow inmate due to be hanged. The work written during his imprisonment was *De Profundis*, published five years later.

> To get a feel for the size of Reading Abbey during its heyday, imagine a church only 50ft shorter than St Paul's Cathedral in London.

The gaol is also adjacent to the Abbey ruins, between the Forbury Gardens Park and the river. Some imagination is needed today to envisage the sheer scale of the Abbey following its growth as a major pilgrimage destination after its consecration by Thomas Beckett in 1164, with the Abbey at one point taking up most of the area covered by the modern town centre.

It is still possible to see St Laurence's church and also the gateway, in the area known to locals as the Butter Market. The church underwent a second phase of building in the fourteenth century and has a number of interesting features including a font by the master mason at Hampton Court Palace that dates back to 1522, choir stalls from slightly earlier and a remnant of the pre-Reformation altar showing the Adoration of the Magi. Look out for the dormitory of the pilgrim's guesthouse of St John the Baptist beside the path through to the graveyard. In the graveyard itself there is also an unusual wooden memorial to a man killed in a whirlwind.

Forbury Gardens occupy the open ground originally owned by the Abbey and used for open air fairs, although the space was contained within the Abbey walls. It survived the rapid growth of the town in modern times as it was bought by the borough for use as a public park in 1835.

> Forbury Gardens was a popular public gathering spot even before they were bought by the Borough. In 1816 crowds came to see Napoleon's military carriage and in 1823 a balloon ascended here to a backdrop of 'God Save the King'. This was also the site of the Cheese Fair, where up to 500 tons of cheese would be exhibited annually until the early 1800s.

It is worth taking one of the Heritage Walks held every Sunday during the summer (see 'Sampling'), but if this is not possible pick up a guide at the Tourist Information Centre and take time to wander around the town where there is much to catch the eye. A few highlights worth mentioning are No.72 London Street, the original home of the Huntley of Huntley & Palmer, famed for their biscuits; the Sun Inn in Castle Street which has a Norman archway that once led to a large underground hall, and the spot behind the Central Library where the original Holy Brook emerges, spanned by the original arch of the Abbey Mill.

Outside Reading, The Most Holy Trinity church in Theale seems dispro-portionately large for such a small town, almost cathedral-like. An early Victorian edifice, the church was built just as Brunel was sur-veying a route for his railway line and reflects the optimism of those times, although it was built in the thirtenth-century early English style with Salisbury Cathedral taken as its model, no less. Particularly worth looking out for is the tower, thought by many to be an afterthought to the original design, and the plastered ceiling, which has a quadripartite vault with ribs decorated by dog-toothing.

John Constable was an early visitor to Theale church and made a sketch of it which now resides in the British Museum.

Padworth College looks impressive but is strictly off-limits, being a girls' boarding school. Padworth's church of St John the Baptist is more welcoming, however, and worth a visit. In the churchyard here there is a 300-year-old yew tree with an inscribed seat dating back to 1907 carrying the message 'Work While 'Tis Day, Then Rest Awhile And Pray.' A modern-looking church with a shingle tower and what looks like a pebble-dashed exterior, the church is said to be one of the smallest in the county. Despite appearances, it dates back to 1130 and features a medieval wall painting of St Nicholas inside.

Finally, Aldermaston Wharf can be reached via footpaths and is particularly notable for its fine example of a scalloped edge lock and the electronically controlled lift bridge that has been known to cause mayhem to local road traffic. Hang around long enough and you might catch a misguided soul who tries to 'rush' it! This is also the site of a Roman Villa, although only the bathhouse survived excavation.

CULTURE AND ENTERTAINMENT

As you might expect, Reading and the surrounding area offer an array of culture and entertainment possibilities. Mention has already been made of the Concert Hall in the Town Hall Complex (01189 606060). Restored in 2000, the venue in fact dates back to 1882 and features traditional U-shaped seating with a surround balcony and a thrust stage, all designed to engineer an intimacy between the audience and performers. A particular feature of the hall is the Father Willis Organ, which booms out from the rear of the stage. The hall hosts a range of entertainment from the expected classical music and organ recitals through to popular music, stand-up comedy and lectures.

Reading is also famous for its Hexagon (01189 606060), known to many of a certain age for its hosting of professional snooker tourna-ments during the 1980s and '90s. These days the venue is put to a variety of uses including rock and pop concerts, comedy, drama, dance and classical music.

A Kennet & Avon welcome sign, Reading.

The South Street Arts Centre (01189 606060) offers both professional and community performing arts and is known for attracting up and coming talents from the fringe theatre, comedy, music, dance and live literature. The venue also hosts the Reading Youth Theatre and the Poets Café, as well as the newly formed Theatre Exchange professional company.

Other venues in the vicinity include the Progress Theatre (01189 606060) which offers high quality amateur theatre with a bias towards the less usual, although they also offer open-air Shakespeare in the grounds of Reading Abbey; and the Rising Sun Arts Centre on Silver Street (01189 866788), a community-based arts centre.

If you are looking to be more energetic there are still plenty of options. The most significant of these is probably the Rivermead Complex (01189 015000) a mile out from the centre of Reading but with grounds stretching down to the Thames. This is a multi-functional centre with two large halls where events as varied as the annual WOMAD Festival of World Music featuring music from more than thirty countries take place, as well as the UK Cheerleading Championships – although not at the same time!

The Rivermead Leisure Complex also has a swimming pool complete with flume and wave machine, a 'Fitness Factory' gym and indoor bowls as well as sports halls. The 13 acres occupied by the Rivermead also acts as the venue for the annual Reading Festival, now firmly established as one of the largest outdoor popular music events in the UK summer circuit, usually held on the last weekend in August. If you are a casual visitor to the town this can be a time to avoid as the transport system and airwaves get taken over by the younger generation.

There is another swimming pool in Battle Street, the Central Pool (01189 015070) which dates back to the 1960s. With four separate pools this probably offers a greater choice to the swimmer than the Rivermead. The South Reading Leisure Centre in Whitley (01189 015040) is a more modern facility with a 25m pool, a sports hall, another gym and a floodlit hardplay area as well as a snooker room. The centre is also host to 'Yippee's Yard', the largest indoor children's play area in the county where there is a maze of play structures and interactive zones.

At Theale Green Recreation Centre (01189 323725) the accent is on fitness with a swimming pool, tennis courts, playing fields and a gymnasium as well as the Berkshire Netball Centre. Equally, despite being one of the oldest of the local sports centres, the Arthur Hill Pool and Fitness Centre on Kings Road (01189 015055) offers not only swimming but circuit training and aerobics.

If your bent is to watch rather than participate in sport the Madejski Stadium (01189 681100) just out off town is fast becoming recognised as one of the south's premier sporting venues and is home to two professional sporting teams, Reading FC and London Irish RFC. There is a match on here most weekends during the season, as well as a variety of other entertainment options.

> Reading FC's record victory was a 10-2 thrashing of Crystal Palace in 1946, although their record defeat was a whopping 18-0 against Preston North End in the first round of the FA Cup way back in 1894.

Other seat-based entertainment includes two cinemas, the Reading Film Theatre within the University (01189 868497) which offers mainly 'art house' cinema, and the more popular Vue Cinema within the Oracle Centre (01189 560047), a ten-screen venue showing all the latest films.

If you need the sun to go down before you begin to relax there is also a good selection of nightlife and bars, mainly within Reading as might be expected given its university status. The following list provides a sample of the places to go, although, as always, tastes may vary:

- 3Bs, Blagrave Street (01189 399803) – *live music, free admission*
- The Afterdark, London Street (01189 576847)
- Bar Med, The Oracle Centre (01189 519990) – *resident DJ*
- Central Club, Duke Street (01189 015644) – *garage, drum 'n' bass*
- Po Na Na, Duke Street (01189 588427)
- Purple Turtle, Gun Street (01189 597196)
- The Jazz Café, Madjeski Stadium (01189 681442) – *club diner, live jazz, funk and soul*
- The Jazz Club, Caversham Road (01189 500950)

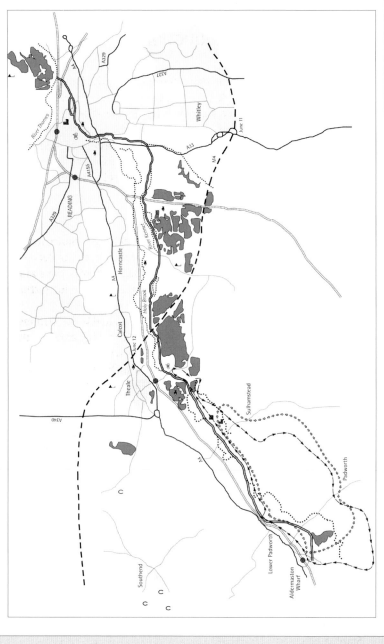

SAMPLING

INTRODUCTION

After a dramatic beginning the canal dips quickly into the open spaces of the Kennet Valley, leaving the buildings of Reading and its suburbs to the north, while a series of large water-filled gravel pits dominate the landscape to the south. Once Theale is passed the area opens up even more, offering an abundance of opportunities to sample the local countryside, either along or away from the towpath.

The OS Explorer Map covering this stretch is No.159, Reading.

WALKING

Other than the Thames Path there are no formal long-distance routes along this section. Heritage walks around the centre of Reading take place every Sunday in the summer months, starting at the statue of Queen Victoria (contact the Tourist Information Centre for further details).

The area also has its fair share of open spaces suitable for walking. One worth mentioning is the Lousehill Copse, hidden away amongst the houses in the northern part of Reading. This is an area of mature woodland including oak and hazel. The copse also includes the Taff Way Woodland, which is a lovely place to see in the spring for its flowers, including bluebells. Blundells Copse above Church End is 13 acres of close-growing ancient woodland complete with a stream, again including mature oak and coppiced hazel, and is also well worth a visit.

Walk A is a mainly field-side and towpath route taking in Padworth and Aldermaston, passing through the wharf at the latter.

SECTION A WALK
From Tyle Mill and Back via Padworth and Aldermaston

Description:	*An easy walk along the floor of the Kennet Valley with a great chance to sample the river and even a salmon ladder*
Distance:	*5 miles*
Duration:	*2hrs*
Starting point:	*Grid Reference 627693, OS Explorer 159*
Nearest refreshment:	*Tea room at the Aldermaston Wharf Visitors' Centre*

From the car park at Tyle Mill turn right, pass over a stream and pick up the footpath on the right just after Rose Court. After a stile stick with the path as it passes through a pasture, a tree nursery and open land, tracking the course of a spring. At the third stile bear slightly left, keeping by a fence and aiming for a makeshift stile in the middle top of the next field.

On reaching a junction take the road heading uphill towards Ufton Court and take the footpath on your right after 100 yards. This cuts across a cultivated field and along the right-hand edge of two more. On meeting a track, bear right and then resume your previous direction along a grassy bank. The path crosses a stream and heads straight out across the following two fields. This ends by becoming a track through trees and comes out on a road where you turn left.

There is no footpath here as the road heads uphill to Padworth. Turn right at the crossroads by a school and pass by Padworth College, following the track on the right that leads down to the church. Go down the footpath on the left and bear right on reaching the road, following

> Look out for the Millennium Salmon Bridge by the Kennet on the walk.

the path as it passes between a house and a barn and along the edge of a horse pasture. Strike out half left after a fence and cross over a stream. Keep straight ahead and cross over another stream and finally the weir carrying the Kennet, the sound of which you will have been hearing for some time.

After the river the path passes down the back of some houses and out onto a track. Turn left here and follow the track down to the road where you are immediately confronted with Aldermaston's (in)famous Lift Bridge. Cross over and pick up the towpath on the right, pausing at the Visitors' Centre if refreshment is required, and head back to Tyle Mill, crossing over the canal at Ufton Bridge.

Walking equipment outlets along this section include:

- Altinus, Oxford Road, Reading (01189 582211)
- Blacks, St Mary's Butts, Reading (01189 595150)
- Carters, Caversham Road, Reading (01189 599022)
- Cotswold Outdoor, Basingstoke Road, Reading (01189 875177)
- Millets, Friar's Walk, Reading (01189 569506)

CYCLING

There is no shortage of cycling routes along this section. The Reading Cyclists' Touring Club (01189 862763) runs regular Wednesday evening rides, normally around 10–15 miles, and the Reading Cycling Campaign (01189 576455) can advise on good cycling routes in the city. Reading Borough Council also produces a map with bike routes through the heart of the built-up area (see 'Learn More and Links').

SECTION A

The first acquaintance is also made here with National Cycle Route 4, which follows the towpath for much of the canal's route.

A recommended cycle route begins at the parking area by Theale Swing Bridge (No.19), from where you head south, turning right at Sheffield Bottom. Follow the road round a sharp turn and pick up the first road on the right, keeping the reservoir to your right. On reaching a road, turn right and then pick up the bridleway immediately on your left and follow this to Uftongreen Farm.

Keep going straight ahead on a road until you reach the Berkshire Circular bridleway on your right after a third of a mile. Follow this to a junction with a footpath where you turn right and then right again on reaching a road. Follow this for another third of a mile and pick up the bridleway on the right at Home Farm.

On reaching a junction of paths, bear right along Fisherman's Lane. This brings you into Aldermaston where you turn right and follow the Basingstoke Road downhill to the canal at Aldermaston Wharf. Pick up the towpath and follow this back to Theale – a total of around 13 miles.

Cycle outlets along this section include:

- Action Bikes, 15 West Street, Reading (01189 511345)
- Berkshire Cycles, Wokingham Road, Reading (01189 661799)
- Blazing Saddles, Prospect Street, Reading (01189 483344)
- Cycology, Loddon Bridge Road, Reading (01189 695776)
- Freewheel, West Street, Reading (01189 510949)
- Halfords (three locations in Reading) (01189 451466)
- Les Smith, London Road, Reading (01189 351564)
- Smiths Cycles, Whitley Wood Lane, Reading (01189 876168)
- Wilkins Cycles, Whitley Street, Reading (01189 871129)

RIDING

This is not an area particularly well-endowed with riding routes. There is some bridleway heading due south from Sulhamstead, to the west of Aldermaston Wharf and around Padworth Common, but little in the way of long-distance routes. This is partly compensated for by a good mix of riding establishments.

Horse-riding establishments and outlets along this section include:

- Bradfield Riding Centre, Bradfield (01189 744048)
- Cullinghood Equestrian Centre, Pangbourne (01189 745228) – complex with two large schools
- Jan Fletcher, Bradfield (01189 744780) – stables and lessons
- Hall Place Equestrian Centre, Tilehurst (01189 426948) – floodlit track, indoor sand school, show jumping paddocks, saddlery
- Oakleigh Grange, Bradfield (01189 744577) – stables

FISHING

Reading and District AA (01189 867430) owns or leases 22 miles of the River Kennet, River Thames, River Loddon and eight stretches of the Kennet & Avon Canal from Bear Wharf Reading to Kennet Junction. The exception is a stretch near Sulhampstead Lock controlled by the Central Association of London and Prov. AA. The RDAA also controls thirteen lakes (see 'Learn More and Links'). The association's waters provide match and pleasure fishing and their website provides an invaluable resource for how to reach their grounds, records and news.

In addition, the Thatcham AA (see Section B) controls a stretch of the Kennet at Padworth which is particularly good for large barbell and carp, along with a few tench and roach which can be fished at Courts Farm Fishery (01932 564872) at Aldermaston. Haywards Farm Lake at Theale (01189 323422) is a purpose-dug trout lake stocked weekly with rainbows.

Finally, the Prospect Angling Club (01189 598457), which is affiliated with the RDAA, has the rights to the Holy Brook at Southcote.

Outlets selling fishing supplies along this stretch include:

- Reading Angling Centre (01189 872216)
- Thames Valley Angling (01189 428249)
- Woodley Sports & Tackle (01189 697907)

> The Holy Brook was dug out by the monks of Reading Abbey in medieval times and flows from the Kennet meadows, under Reading town centre and back into the Kennet by the Abbey ruins.

In addition, the Sportfish Fly Fishing Centre near Theale (01189 303860) offers tuition in the mysteries of fly fishing as well as a full range of fly fishing equipment.

OTHER

This is an area well blessed with golfing opportunities. The following list sets out the main courses along this section:

- Calcot Park Golf Club, Calcot (01189 427124) – *6,216-yard, 18-hole, par-70 course set in mature woodland and countryside*
- Dog Golf Course, Reading (01189 344355) – *9 hole*
- Hurst Golf Club, Twyford (01189 344355) – *9 hole*
- Reading Golf Club (01189 472909) – *north of the town centre, 6,088-yard, 18-hole, par-70 course*
- Rivermead Golf Driving Range (01189 504343) – *39-bay floodlit driving range with target greens and golf shop*
- Theale Golf Centre (01189 305331) – *6,395-yard, 18-hole, par-72 parkland course*

ALDERMASTON WHARF TO MARSH BENHAM

CAUTION
CROSS CURRENT
FROM LEFT
LOW ARCHED
BRIDGE AHEAD

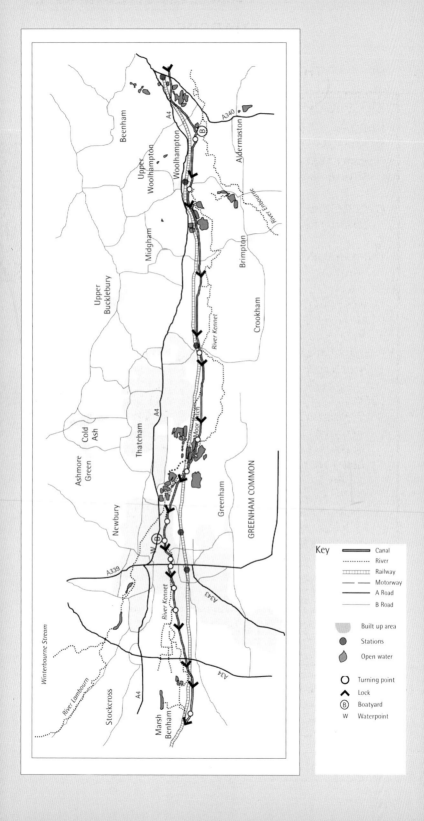

Key

Canal
River
Railway
Motorway
A Road
B Road

Built up area
Stations
Open water
O   Turning point
⌃   Lock
Ⓑ   Boatyard
W   Waterpoint

SHAPERS

THE CANAL ON THIS STRETCH

KEY FACTS

LENGTH: 10¼ miles

BOATYARDS: 2
Froud's Bridge Marina
Newbury Boat Co.

WATERPOINTS: 1
Newbury Boat Co.

TURNING POINTS: 12

Froud's Bridge Marina Approach	Greenham Lock
Heale's Lock	Greenham Bridge
Monkey Marsh	Newbury Wharf
Moor Ditch	West Mills
Bull's Bridge	West Fields
Ham Marsh	Marsh Benham

LOCKS: 15

Aldermaston Lock (6ft 11in)	Bull's Lock (5ft 9in)
Woolhampton (8ft 11in)	Ham Lock (4ft 2in)
Heale's Lock (8ft 11in)	Greenham Lock (6ft 11in)
Midgham Lock (7ft 9in)	Newbury Lock (5ft 3in)
Colthrop Lock (7ft 7in)	Guyer's Lock (7ft 0in)
Monkey Marsh Lock (6ft 8in)	Higg's Lock (5ft 10in)
Widmead Lock (3ft 7in)	Benham Lock (6ft 3in)
	Hamstead Lock (6ft 5in)

Punctuated by Newbury, this stretch sees the canal hitting its stride, with turf-sided locks and the growing presence of the railway, as the route flits in between open land and woods. There is also a fair quotient of swing bridges of varying degrees of difficulty.

Aldermaston Lock is a gem. With its scalloped sides and useful information board sitting above the town, it is worth visiting in its own right. A welcome stretch with a couple of lock-free miles follows, although the obstacle waiting at the end is both formidable and notorious. But before then, there is a pair of long straights with the river now flowing to the south and the railway coming so close it is almost possible to touch it.

The course becomes a meandering river again shortly after Fround's Bridge, flowing through deep woods, although the railway continues to lurk behind the trees and, as if in response, the towpath crosses to the other side at the delightful dark brick and wood Wickham Knight footbridge.

The aforementioned obstacle now looms, the dreaded Woolhampton combination of swing bridge, lock and strong river current, after which it may be a relief to learn there are some 48-hour moorings for those needing to regain their confidence, as well as their breath!

Oxlease and Cranwell's swing bridges need windlasses to remove a restraining pin and in between the two bridges is Heale's Lock, at nearly 9ft one of the deepest on this run, soon followed by Midgham and Colthrop Locks, both 7ft plus.

The recommended approach to Woolhampton is, when approaching upstream, to set the lock before opening the bridge and then to head straight into the current, turning into the lock at the final moment.

After these, the scenery becomes more commercial in nature, although the river can still be seen in the distance to the left, with the canal again adopting its more man-made straight appearance. Willow trees dangle their fingertips into the water on the non-towpath side. Thatcham Station sits right alongside the canal and provides a good access point.

Another turf-sided lock follows at Monkey Marsh, followed by a further long straight and Widmead and Bull Lock. Ham Lock, half a mile further on, marks the beginning of Newbury proper, and although there is a turning point just after it, this can be a tricky one to negotiate owing to the current flowing down to a weir to the north.

An attractive wooden bridge carries the towpath over to the right before Greenham Lock, which in turn precedes the Newbury Boat Co. (01635 42884), where there are the usual facilities, including water and pump out, as well as another bridge allowing access to the shop at the marina.

The marina acts as an introduction to the landscaped sweep the canal takes through the centre of Newbury, with the townspeople quite rightly regarding the waterway as an asset and a main thoroughfare, with a pedestrianised towpath.

A couple of low bridges in the heart of Newbury effectively limit the height of craft that can negotiate the canal to 7ft.

Bars and parks line the side and there is a park on the left with a boating lake with its own version of watercraft. The Kennet darts in and out of the canal, disappearing for a while in a run off just before Newbury Lock, and boaters need to be careful if taking advantage of the temporary mooring as the current can be quite tricky.

Newbury ends with the pretty West Mills area, where the buildings belie the area's name and there is an electricity-operated swing bridge followed by moorings. The towpath swaps over here to the left. An unusual high-arched metal pipe and footbridge follows, guarded by an old concrete pill box, something of a feature of this stretch of canal.

The towpath swaps back over to the right at Guyer's Lock just out of town, and the landscape here is a contrast of farmland and woods on one side and marshland pockmarked with willows on the other, with the railway in the near distance sitting on an embankment. This is a quiet and picturesque stretch and leads up to a classic bridge and lock scene at Benham after another long straight guarded by yet more redundant pill boxes. Between Benham and Hamstead locks, the river widens out for a while and becomes almost Thames-like in its appearance, complete with its own weir.

PRINCIPAL TOWNS AND VILLAGES ALONG THIS STRETCH

ALDERMASTON
Forever linked with the notorious Weapons Establishment that bears its name (referred to, rather ominously, as AWE), this lies a couple of miles to the south of the village, which bears visiting in its own right for its elegant red-brick housing with intricate brickwork. The village dates back to medieval times and is home to Aldermaston Court.

ASHMORE GREEN
Effectively part of nearby Cold Ash, the tree mentioned features in many Berkshire place names as it was sacred to the Saxon God Woden.

BEENHAM
A spread-out village with a vineyard on its edge, Beenham is split between one half alongside the A4 and the original focus on the side of the Kennet Valley. The church and playground provide some focus, as the common which might otherwise have done so appears rather unloved.

BRIMPTON
Brimpton enjoys impressive views out over the Kennet Valley and has a grandiose village hall on its outskirts. Evidence of Bronze Age round barrows can be seen to the south and the local church once had Roman tiles on its walls.

COLD ASH
A collection of mostly quite well-to-do housing and estates developed in the 1950s and '60s, Cold Ash exists as a village outpost of Newbury.

CROOKHAM
A small hamlet on the edge of the common that bears its name with a pub, a couple of farms and a caravan park as well as a handful of houses.

> Newbury was renamed Kennetbridge by Thomas Hardy in *Jude the Obscure*, with Jude visiting the town to call on the composer of a hymn that had got stuck in his mind.

GREENHAM
Best known for its nearby airbase, Greenham has a long and distinguished history.

MARSH BENHAM
A handful of well-to-do houses sitting by the canal and river, the most significant of which is Craven House.

MIDGHAM
An undistinguished village sitting on the side of the Kennet Valley overlooked by Midgham Park and the domineering spire of St Matthew's church visible from miles around, including from the towpath.

NEWBURY
'New' because it predates Domesday, Newbury sits at the junction of the east/west A4 and the north/south A34 and remains a vibrant and important stopping point.

STOCKCROSS
A well-kept village bisected by the B4000 with the church, manor and village hall on one side of the road and housing on the other, along with a large nursing home.

> Three Thatcham residents have won the Victoria Cross, two of them brothers, one in each of the two world wars, whilst the third was won in the Boer War.

THATCHAM
The scene of a lot of recent, and continuing, development, Thatcham is mentioned in the *Guinness Book of Records* as the oldest continuously inhabited place in England.

UPPER BUCKLEBURY
Sitting on the edge of its common, Upper Bucklebury is a dispersed village with mostly modern housing acting as a dormitory to nearby Newbury.

UPPER WOOLHAMPTON
Douai Abbey, a Benedictine priory with a school attached, sits perched on the hill and these, along with another school to the south, basically constitute Upper Woolhampton.

WOOLHAMPTON
Straddling the A4, Woolhampton's station bears the name of nearby Midgham. A collection of old and new cottages line the road to the canal, with the latter sympathetically, and at times eccentrically, blended in. The twin obstacles of a level crossing and a lift bridge can make progress slow on the road heading south.

> It was in Woolhampton that the highwayman Captain Hawkes was captured. Known for his disguises, he was somewhat cheekily dressed as a Quaker when caught.

HISTORY

This part of West Berkshire has been a popular spot to settle for millennia. Dating back to Mesolithic times, evidence has been found of temporary settlements, including hearths and flint and bone tools as well as animal remains (including elk and wolves).

Evidence of later Bronze Age settlement still exists in Brimpton to the south, where there are five round barrows (known as the Borson Barrows). These remained significant until Saxon times and were noted as boundary markers in a charter dated AD944.

> The skeleton of a Roman man, complete with his horse and chariot, has been found at Colthrop Mill, the suggestion being that he plunged into nearby marshes, one of the country's earliest documented traffic victims!

Before then the Romans were the first to establish themselves on any scale, with Thatcham a chosen spot. Evidence exists of houses spread out along a section of the Ermine Way linking Cirencester and Silchester, near to the modern Bath Road. Most significantly, the Romans are thought to have built a bridge over the Kennet here, rather than their usual ford. Again, this was mentioned in a Saxon charter where it was referred to as 'Welshman's Bridge', suggesting a Romano-Briton origin.

Thatcham was a small-scale industrial area in Roman times, with digs revealing pieces of bronze, iron slag and coal. Further evidence of Roman settlement includes the fourth-century bathhouse at Beenham, an impressive structure with its own hypocaust.

Next came the Saxons, who sailed up the Thames and Kennet and adopted some of the abandoned Roman settlements. Thatcham church, known to date from around this time, was founded by St Birinus in the seventh century. Ashmore Green's name is also thought to be of Saxon origin, as is Woolhampton's, which was originally known as Ollavintone.

After the Saxons came the Normans, who were to have a significant impact on the area by establishing the town of Newbury. This was the work of Arnulf De Hesdin just after the Conquest, with Newbury being one of a number of new towns established by the Normans to act as centres of commerce and industry and, indirectly, swell the coffers of the local lords.

Newbury had its own castle a century later. Not much to be proud of, despite being featured on the town's day coat of arms, this was besieged by King Stephen but today no trace of it remains. King John visited in 1200, establishing St Bartholomew's Hospital. He is also thought to have hidden from the rebel barons chasing him in the town, sequestered away by an old spinning woman.

As Newbury grew in stature, so its ancient rivalry with nearby Thatcham began to take root. At the time of the Conquest, Thatcham was second only to Windsor in the Berkshire hundreds. In 1125 the

SECTION B

manor was granted to Reading Abbey by Henry I, a status that allowed it to hold a Sunday market in the church. When Henry II confirmed the market it was too much for the good folk of Newbury who promptly marched over and smashed the market up.

Thatcham's commercial peak was reached in the early fourteenth century when it was one of the four boroughs of Berkshire, but it never really recovered from the devastation of the Black Death. Meanwhile, other pockets of power sprang up, including the manor of Greenham, which was owned by the Knights Hospitaller from 1199 and was the order's main base in the county.

Newbury continued to grow, not least off the back of wool, but suffered from backing the rebel Duke of York during the Wars of the Roses. Taken by the Duke of Wiltshire, many of the town's inhabitants suffered the ignominy of being hanged, drawn and quartered.

The path to future prosperity had been found, though, and before long Newbury became known as the cloth-trading capital of the south. This was due in no small part to the entrepreneurial skills of John Winchcombe, known as Jack O'Newbury, a runaway who married his boss's widow and went on to build what has some claims to be the country's first factory. Evidence of the town's debt to wool is still visible today, including the museum which is housed in a three-storey Jacobean building with a first-floor overhang.

> Jack and his son John Winchcombe were responsible for rebuilding St Nicholas' church. Their insignia can be seen in the roof bosses.

Although it may be tempting to see the influence of sheep in Woolhampton's name, this was not the case. Greenham, however, was a wool centre and the famous Newbury Coat was made at Greenham Mills. What made this coat so special was that it was manufactured in 13 hours and 20 minutes – from a sheep's back to a man's.

Around this time Newbury's supremacy over Thatcham became complete when Jack Winchcombe's descendants were granted the manor of Thatcham upon the Dissolution. The lands were divided into two, with one passing in time to General Waring who built Dunstan House and planted the grounds with trees placed in accordance with troop placements from battles he had fought.

The Civil War left its mark upon this area, with two battles being fought at Newbury. Initially coming out for Parliament, the town fell to the king but was retaken by the Parliamentary forces when the Royalists ran out of gunpowder. Troops were stationed around a number of the villages along this stretch, including Beenham.

> Beenham's church has suffered a number of fires over the years. After one in 1794 the villagers rescued enough bell metal to reduce the cost of recasting the six bells – the local pub taking the name The Six Bells in recognition of this feat.

With peace, the area's natural advantages came back to favour it, not least its prominent position on the Bath Road, which became the

Newbury High Street.

scene of long wagon trains in the sixteenth century. In later years this led to the establishment of a number of coaching inns. Woolhampton, Thatcham and Newbury all benefited from their positions on the road, an advantage that redoubled with the coming of the turnpikes and improved roads.

The Kennet Navigation opened in 1723, with the full Kennet & Avon Canal following in 1810. All was not sweetness and light, however, with the Swing Riots discussed in Section A also having a profound impact along this stretch, with Newbury the base from which the authorities set out from to suppress the mayhem.

In more recent times both Greenham and Newbury have hit the international headlines, the former as the US army base where cruise missiles were stationed and the latter through protests at the building of the town's bypass. These days the bypass is complete, with the head-quarters of the UK's largest company, Vodafone, a prominent feature. Even Thatcham seems to have recovered and claims to be the country's fastest growing town, although there seems to be a number of contend-ers for this dubious crown.

THE NATURAL LANDSCAPE

The Kennet Valley dominates the landscape along the southern part of this stretch, with gentle countryside populated by willows sitting by the side of expansive meadows. The two great commons of Bucklebury and Greenham punctuate the landscape to the north and south respectively, with further woodland lining the towpath after Newbury to the west.

The Kennet is joined by the Lambourn, known for its trout, in Newbury by Ham Lock, and there is further water to the east of the town including a nature reserve and the Jubilee Centre Discovery Centre, as well as lakes sitting by the side of Newbury Race Course. A steep rise to the north at Woolhampton means the railway and canal have to squeeze together to avoid a climb.

ACCESS AND TRANSPORT

ROADS
Having joined the towpath at Aldermaston, the A4 now becomes a near constant companion to the canal through this and the following section. Here it links Aldermaston with Woolhampton, Thatcham and Newbury. The A340 makes a brief appearance from the south through Aldermaston, manifesting as a lift bridge over the canal just north of the town.

Newbury acts as the main road hub in this section, with the A339 passing north to south through the town and the A343 spurring off to the south-west. Further to the east, the A34 provides another north–south route bypassing the centre. Newbury, Thatcham and Woolhampton all provide good road access to the canal, with parking just south of the canal at the latter.

Minor roads cross the canal at Midgham to the east of Woolhampton and again west of the village. Such roads tend to be more prolific to the north of the canal, with the Kennet's valley continuing to provide a natural barrier to the south in the earlier stages of this section, although a long east/west route links the A339 and Aldermaston.

> The station in Woolhampton is named after a neighbouring village, Midgham, because of early confusion with Wolverhampton, presumably more by rail staff than passengers.

RAIL
This section is well blessed with rail stations, with stops at Midgham (Woolhampton), Thatcham, Newbury and Newbury Racecourse. Services are operated by First Great Western Link (08457 484950) providing a mainly commuter service to London.

For more detailed information contact National Train Enquiries on 08457 484950 or www.nationalrail.co.uk.

BUSES
The following list sets out the main bus services for this section although it is advisable to check before using them as some buses only run on certain days and others may have been withdrawn since publication of this Guide. It is also worth checking for more local services, especially in the Newbury area, where there are both circular and school term-time services.

- 3A, 3B, 3C – *Newbury circular local service (Reading Buses)*
- 4 – *Newbury to Lambourn via Greenham and Stockcross*
- *(Reading Buses)*
- 10/12 – *Thatcham to Newbury via Greenham (Reading Buses)*
- 15 – *Newbury circular local*

service (Reading Buses)

- 32 – *Newbury to Basingstoke via Greenham (Reading Buses)*
- 32a – *Newbury to Basingstoke via Greenham (Hampshire Bus)*
- 73 – *Beenham to Reading via Aldermaston and Padworth Common. Wednesdays only. (Four Valleys)*
- 95 – *Baydon to Newbury via Marsh Benham. Thursday only (Collins)*
- 101/102 – *Newbury to Reading via Thatcham, Woolhampton and Theale (Reading Buses)*

- 103 – *Reading to Newbury, via Theale, Woolhampton and Thatcham (Reading Buses)*
- 104/105 – *Newbury to Calcot via Brimpton, Aldermaston, Beenham and Theale (Reading Buses)*
- 118 – *Newbury to Beenham. Thursdays only (Reading Buses)*
- C21/22 – *Newbury Circular (Hampshire Bus)*
- X8 – *links Newbury, Thatcham and Cold Ash (Weavaway Travel)*

In addition, the National Express coach service 402 links Trowbridge, Melksham, Devizes, Hungerford and Newbury on its way into London once every day of the week, passing through a number of the sections covered in this Guide.

Contact details for bus operators in this area are listed below, although Traveline (www.traveline.org.uk) on 0870 6082608 can give details of specific services between 7 a.m. and 10 p.m.:

- Collins, Newbury (0789 9044304)
- Four Valleys Minibus Services, Newbury (01635 35806)
- Hampshire Bus, Basingstoke (01256 464501)

- National Express, Birmingham (08705 808080)
- Reading Buses, Reading (0118 9594000)
- Weavaway, Newbury (01635 820028)

TAXIS

The following list gives a selection of the taxi operators in this section:

- A2B Taxis, Thatcham (01635 877777)
- Abacus Cars, Thatcham (01635 582226)
- Alpha Cars, Thatcham (01635 866777)
- Am Pam Cars, Newbury (01635 48473)
- Axis Cars, Newbury (07950 312245)
- Cabco, Newbury (01635 33333)

- Dolphin Taxis, Thatcham (01635 862832)
- Kingfisher Taxis, Newbury (01635 30312)
- Newbury Taxis, Newbury (01635 34444)
- JDM Taxis, Thatcham (01635 826763)
- Williams Taxis, Thatcham (01635 869541)

SECTION A   READING TO ALDERMASTON LOCK

This page, top, and opposite: *Aldermaston Lock.*

This page, bottom: *Reading's Coat of Arms.*

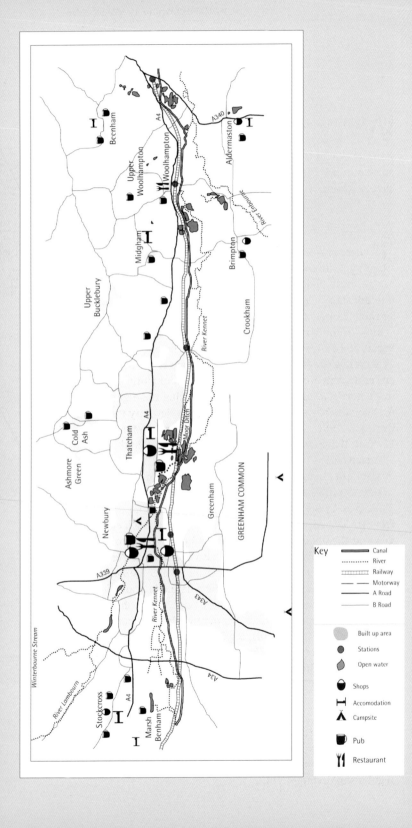

Key

	Canal
	River
	Railway
	Motorway
	A Road
	B Road

Built up area

Stations

Open water

Shops

Accomodation

Campsite

Pub

Restaurant

BASICS

INTRODUCTION

Whilst the near neighbours of Thatcham and Newbury dominate the centre of this section they are surrounded by a number of smaller villages. Although many of these have their own pub, few have much to offer in the way of shopping or restaurants, which seem to have migrated to the two larger towns.

SHOPPING

Thatcham and Newbury share the honours for being the main shopping centres along this section. Although Newbury is more comprehensive and modern, Kennet Shopping Centre has recently undergone a refurbishment and has a Marks and Spencer as well as a number of smaller, more niche, outlets.

Most of the large High Street names have selected Newbury as their venue, and there is also a department store here as well as a Tesco Metro by the car park. The department store, Camp Hopson, is Newbury's own rather than part of a chain. It is also worth exploring some of the side roads here leading off to the canal, including the Eight Bells Shopping Arcade, which has mainly antiques. Also in Newbury there is the Kennet Centre, a small mall. Newbury holds a Farmer's Market in the Market Place on the morning of the first Sunday every month.

Thatcham has the Kingsland Shopping Centre, with a Waitrose supermarket on the edge by a car park. Also included in the centre is a not hugely inspiring assortment of bakers, travel agents and charity shops. There is a Co-op on the High Street as well as the usual small-town facilities including banks and restaurants, all of which enclose a pleasant green in the middle, breaking it up and giving more of a small-village feel. Wines, cheeses and fruits are also available at Westbury Wines at Lower Henwick Farm outside Thatcham (01635 869760), and the Kiln Fold at Midgham (01189 712138) offers naturally reared beef.

Elsewhere, Aldermaston Stores has a basic village shop and the village also has an antique shop and a pottery whilst Woolhampton has a shop called Magic and Fairy Tails, a gift and fairy shop, along with a newsagent and a post office attached to The Angel pub. Finally, there is a small village store at Brimpton (Forge Stores) and another in Stockcross.

EATING AND DRINKING

This is an area unusually well endowed with places to feed and water, many of which are within striking distance of the towpath, while the A4 continues to betray its coaching route past by having a regular smattering of pubs.

SECTION A   READING TO ALDERMASTON WHARF

Above: *The Oracle Centre, Reading.*

Opposite above: *Aldermaston Lock.*
Opposite below: *Reading Abbey and gaol.*

- The Six Bells, Beenham (01189 713368)
- The Winning Hand, Beenham (01189 302472)
- The Angel, Woolhampton (01189 713307) – *also has a restaurant*
- Falmouth Arms, Woolhampton (01189 713202)
- The Rising Sun, Upper Woolhampton (01189 712717) – *on A4*
- The Row Barge, Woolhampton (01189 712213) – *canalside*
- The Coach and Horses, Midgham (01189 713384)
- The Three Horseshoes, Brimpton (01189 712183)
- Travellers Friend, Brimpton (01189 713156)
- The Cottage Inn, Upper Bucklebury (01635 864544)
- The Bunk Inn, Thatcham (01635 200400)
- The Cricketers, Thatcham (01635 862113)
- The Old Chequers, Thatcham (01635 861233)
- The Kings Head, Thatcham (01635 862145)
- The Swan, Thatcham (01635 40313) – *pub and restaurant*
- The Wheatsheaf, Thatcham (01635 862670)
- The Castle, Cold Ash (01635 863232)
- The Spotted Dog, Cold Ash (01635 862458)
- Broadways, Newbury (01635 523030)
- The Bowler's Arms, Newbury (01635 47658)
- The Catherine Wheel, Newbury (01635 47471)
- The Hatchet, Newbury (01635 47352)
- The Kings Head, Newbury (01635 862145)
- The Lamb Inn, Newbury (01635 40912)
- Lock Stock and Barrel, Newbury (01635 580550) – *right by the lock*
- The Old Wagon and Horses, Newbury (01488 658215) – *canalside bar*
- Sun in the Wood, Newbury (01635 42377)
- Uncle Henry's, Newbury (01635 523249)
- The White House, Newbury (01635 42614)
- The Lord Lyon, Stockcross (01488 608366)
- The Halfway Inn (01488 658215) – *between Newbury and Hungerford on the A4*

> The Chef's Launch (01635 42231) is a 62ft narrowboat based in Newbury which can be hired out for gourmet meals.

- The Hare and Hounds (01635 521152) – *on A4 between Newbury and Stockcross*
- Rising Sun, Stockcross (01488 608131)
- The Red House, Marsh Benham (01635 582017)

As with shopping, Newbury is the main place to head if it is variety of restaurants you are after, with Newbury again the focus for the large national chains, along with Thatcham, around which there is a reasonable range of restaurants. There is plenty more on offer elsewhere, however, with many of the plentiful pubs offering a serendipitous feast, so it is worth exploring.

The following selection offers a sample of restaurants in and around Newbury:

- Gordons, Cheap Street (01635 31274) – *restaurant and bar*
- Eight Bells Café and Bistro (01635 35003) – *British*
- Indigo Bay, Barthelomew Street (01635 35000) – *Indian*
- Khan Tandoori, The Broadway (01635 47499) – *Indian*
- Laurel Peking Cuisine, Cheap Street (01635 44299) – *Chinese*
- The Square Bar and Grill, Northbrook Street (01635 44805) – *International*
- Valle D'Oro (01635 47428) – *Italian*

Newbury also offers an excellent selection of cafés and snack bars, including:

- Alfie's Café, The Broadway (01635 865511)
- Alfredos Tapas Bar, Bartholomew Street (01635 40162)
- Boswell's Coffee House, Kennet Shopping Centre (01635 521122)
- Camp Hopson, Northbrook Street (01635 523523) – *in the department store*
- Empire Café, Cheap Street (01635 41424)
- Out to Lunch, Market Place (01635 581591)
- Scoffers, Northbrook Street (01635 230680)
- Weavers Coffee Shop, Northbrook Street (01635 528018)

In addition, the Kennet & Avon Canal Trust offers a selection of food at its café at The Stone Building in Newbury (01635 522609) opposite the Tourist Information Centre.

Restaurants around Thatcham include:

- The Bunk Inn, Curridge (01635 200400) – *British*
- Hussain's, The Broadway (01635 868800) – *Indian*
- Jade Cottage, High Street (01635 861880) – *Peking and Thai*
- The Mandarin Court, The
- Broadway (01635 874019) – *Chinese*
- Taste of England, Turnpike Road (01635 869760) – *British*
- Thatcham Tandoori and Balti,
- The Broadway (01635 876203) – *Indian*

There is also a good selection of cafés around Thatcham, including:

- Arts Centre Café, Greenham (01635 581858)
- Café Delice, Kingsland Centre
- (01635 867229)
- Forge Coffee Shop, The Broadway (01635 865127)

SECTION B   ALDERMASTON TO MARSH BENHAM

Top: *One of the many bridges crossing the River Kennet.*
Above: *Newbury Lock.*

Top: *Monkey Marsh Lock.*

Above left: *Newbury Corn Exchange.*
Above right: *Newbury Kennet & Avon Trust Shop.*

SLEEPING

The A4 and the proximity to Reading mean that there are plenty of places to stay along this section, covering most price brackets.

- The Berkshire Arms, Woolhampton (0118 9714114)
- West Grange Hotel, Midgham (01635 862351)
- Regency Park, Thatcham (01635 871555)
- Chequers Hotel, Newbury (0870 6096141)
- Hare and Hounds Hotel and Restaurant, Newbury (01635 521152)
- The Newbury Manor Hotel (01635 528838)
- The Queens Hotel, Newbury (0870 3305147)
- Ramada Hotel and Resort, Elcot Park (01488 658100) – *luxury resort hotel between Hungerford and Newbury*
- The Vineyard, Stockcross (01635 528770)

HOTELS

- The Six Bells, Beenham (01189 713368)
- **The Hinds Head, Aldermaston village (**01189 712194)
- Eastfield, Midgham (01189 713160)
- Highwood View, Midgham (01189 713098)

The West Mills area of Newbury.

Victoria Park Bridge.

- 55 Chapel Street, Thatcham (01635 861000)
- The White Hart, Thatcham (01635 863251)
- Bacon Arms, Newbury (01635 31822)
- East End Farm, Newbury (01635 254895)
- Ingledene Bed and Breakfast, Newbury (01635 43622)
- The Limes Guest House, Newbury (01635 33082)
- The Pilgrim's Guest House, Newbury (01635 232425)
- Livingstone House, Newbury (01635 45444)
- The Old Plough, North End, Newbury (01635 254769)
- Rookwood Farmhouse, Stockcross (01488 608676)

BED AND BREAKFAST/GUEST HOUSES
CAMPING

- Bishops Green Farm, Newbury (01635 268365) – *30 pitches and hook ups in 50 acres of woodland*
- Oakley Farm Caravan Park,

Newbury (01635 36581) – *30 pitches for tents, caravans and motor caravans within a 3-acre farm site*

There are two significant caravan and camping sites in this section: The nearest camping supplies outlet in this section is:
- Millets, Newbury (01635 40070)

SECTION B   ALDERMASTON TO MARSH BENHAM

Top: *Newbury Trip Boat.*
Above: *Newbury Museum.*

Opposite top: *Woolhampton.*
Opposite below: *Newbury Lock and Bridge.*

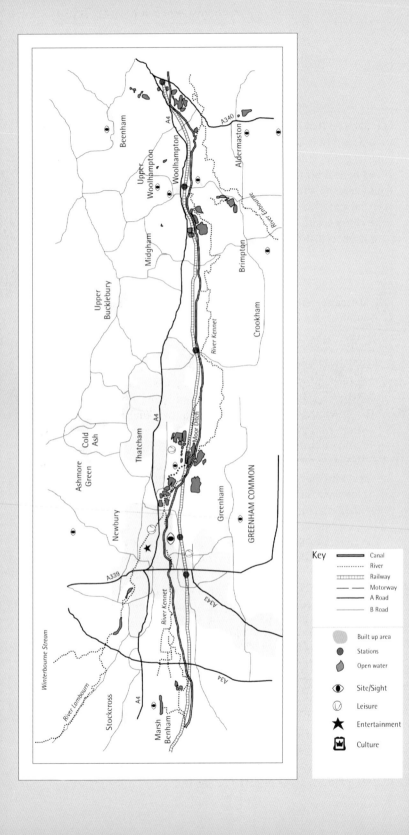

Key

	Canal
	River
	Railway
	Motorway
	A Road
	B Road

Built up area

Stations

Open water

Site/Sight

Leisure

Entertainment

Culture

SEEING AND DOING

INTRODUCTION

Although Thatcham is a reasonably sized town it offers little to the casual visitor in the way of historical or cultural sustenance. Its more modern feel is reflected in the fact that it is home to two more themed attractions, whilst it is left to Newbury to provide more traditional attractions along this stretch. Many of the surrounding villages are also worth a visit and a number of sites within these are listed below.

Newbury is also home to the local Tourist Information Centre situated on the wharf (01635 30267).

SIGHTS

Aldermaston sits on the edge of the famous weapons establishment, although the fences do not detract too much if you decide to stick in the centre of the village. Here the gates of Portland House dominate but they are not the originals – they were won in a card game from the owners of nearby Midgham House.

> Aldermaston is one of the few places that still holds a candle auction. A pin is placed an inch from the flame of a tallow candle and bidding continues until the pin falls with the last bid before it falls securing the lot – here the three-year lease of a field called Church Acre.

The church was a Saxon minster and contains an alabaster effigy of Sir George Foster, the local lord, and his wife, dating back to 1530. The Fosters also live on in the name of the Hinds Head pub, named after the Fosters' crest. The pub has its own gaol house round the back, so it would be wise to be on your best behaviour if you decide to stop for a drink.

The church of St Mary's at Beenham has suffered a number of fires over the years, which means that few of its thirteenth-century origins are still visible. Inside there is a memorial to Sir Charles Hopson, who was knighted by Queen Anne and was notable for being the man responsible for much of the woodwork in St Paul's Cathedral.

> Beenham was also the church of Thomas Stackhouse, a theologian who wrote the grandly titled *New History of the Holy Bible from the Beginning of the World until the Coming of Christianity* in 1937. Perhaps ironically, much of this was said to be have written at a pub in nearby Sulhamstead.

There is little to see at Woolhampton, although this was not always the case. Before being rebuilt in 1857, the church of St Peter was said to have a twelfth-century carved font featuring lead figures depicting saints, with St Peter himself shown with a book and a key. Rumour has it that this figure is buried beneath the floor of the church although it has never been found.

SECTION C   MARSH BENHAM TO CROFTON

Top: *Great Bedwyn church.*
Above left: *Froxfield Somerset Hospital gateway.*
Above right: *Great Bedwyn Stores with memorials.*

Opposite top: *Crofton – railway, canal and Wilton Water.*
Opposite below: *Great Bedwyn thatched cottages.*

SECTION B

Although there is little formal to see it is worth taking the time to linger a little in Woolhampton, perhaps after a leisurely pint at one of its pubs. There are a few architectural curiosities here such as a house with its own tower and another with a clock built into its side; these are unusual because both are clearly modern builds. There is also a drinking fountain on the corner with the A4, erected to celebrate Queen Victoria's Golden Jubilee.

Douai Abbey in Upper Woolhampton (01189 715300) is a community of Benedictine monks offering a mix of courses and retreats and its Abbey church is often used as a venue for choral, orchestral and chamber concerts. The order originated in France but decamped to Woolhampton in 1903 when the political situation made it impossible for them to continue their work in that country. Until recently there was also a school here but this closed in 1999, with the buildings being redeveloped as private housing.

Bucklebury Farm Park (01189 714002) north of Woolhampton offers the opportunity to see wild boar, Red, Fallow and Sika Deer as well as to pat-a-pet and feed the animals. It also has an outdoor adventure playground, picnic area and refreshments.

Five Bronze Age barrows are visible to the south of Brimpton. Known as the 'Borson Barrows', these are thought to be boundary markers noted in a Saxon charter dated 944. Whilst in Brimpton, look out also for the farmhouse, once known as Brimpton Court, which is surrounded by the remains of a thirteenth-century moat. The house also has a priest hole in the dining room, which was only discovered in the 1960s, although without any occupants.

The main attraction in the Thatcham area is the Thatcham Nature Discovery Centre (01635 874381). This is described as offering an exploration into the natural world and the environment for all the family. The attraction includes a Nature Discovery Hall complete with interactive exhibits, along with giant models of insects, an exhibition gallery and two large children's playgrounds alongside a lakeside café. If you over-indulge in the latter there is also a series of walks around the lake and reedbeds, complete with a bird hide.

It was not that long ago that the thought of recommending Greenham Common as a local attraction would have been a perverse suggestion. Associated throughout the world with protest against nuclear weapons, the common, along with the adjacent Crookham Common, has been returned to public use and amply justifies a mention as a place worth visiting. A very good website (see 'Learn More and Links') provides a visitors' guide to how to get the best out of these heathlands.

Bowdown Woods Nature Reserve, incorporating Baynes Reserve, is managed by the Berks, Bucks & Oxon Wildlife Trust. This lies between the two commons and incorporates mature oak and ash woodlands along with woodland indicators such as herb paris, common solomon's seal and moschatel – sometimes known as town hall clock flower. The reserve is also said to be home to 300 different types of fungi, so get counting.

The Kennet flows through the centre of Newbury and provides a good focal point for the town, popping up regularly as you wander around its streets. There are plenty of historic buildings, mainly from the seventeenth and eighteenth centuries, and the wharf with nearby car park and park linked via a bridge is a popular gathering point. This is also the site of the Kennet & Avon Trust's shop and mini-exhibition (01635 522609) housed in the Stone Building, the last remnant of a complex of wharfside buildings.

The West Mills area on the way out of the town is also picturesque, mainly because of its waterside buildings. The Corn Exchange in the centre of town, meanwhile, is a popular arts venue and provides a contrast to the pre-industrial tone of many of Newbury's older buildings, being noticeably nineteenth century in origin, although built in the Italianate style.

St Nicholas' also has a memorial tablet dedicated to John and Frances West, genealogists who left an endowment at Christ's Hospital for the education of children from Newbury.

Other buildings to look out for include St Nicholas school and the church sharing its name. The latter was built just as the town was reaching its peak of wealth as a wool town and this is clear in its grandeur, at least from the outside. Inside, the church is more modest, with most of the 'popish' fittings removed by Cromwell and his men when they used the church as a 'one stop' stable, hospital and prison during the first Battle of Newbury.

If visiting the church look out for the Jacobean pulpit and sounding board which dates back to 1607, and the font, which has such a heavy cover that there is a chained mechanism to lift it. Also, see if you can spot the 'Blue Coat Boy' who advertised the poor box which collected funds for the local Blue Coat School.

Newbury's West Berkshire Museum (01635 30511) is housed in seventeenth- and eighteenth-century buildings and has over 200,000 exhibits. Entrance is free, so it does not matter if you have to make a return visit to view it all.

Donnington Castle, north of Newbury, is a ruin, torn down after the Second Battle of Newbury during the Civil War in 1644, which took place around the castle. That said, there is still much to see including a twin-towered gatehouse and sufficient earthworks to allow you to imagine what it originally looked like. Owned by English Heritage, admission is free here also.

Tucked away between Newbury and Marsh Benham lies Benham Park, an eighteenth-century manor house with Capability Brown gardens, including a water feature that harnesses the Kennet. The modern house shows signs of enlargement during the Victorian period and these days the house is used as offices.

SECTION B

SECTION C   MARSH BENHAM TO CROFTON

Top: *Kintbury and a horse-drawn boat.*
Above: *Kintbury.*

Opposite top: *Hungerford – the view from the lock.*
Opposite middle: *Kintbury Vicarage.*
Opposite bottom: *Little Bedwyn.*

Monkey Marsh Lock.

CULTURE AND ENTERTAINMENT

Newbury acts as the main entertainment focus in this section. The Corn Exchange (01635 522733) offers a varied programme of entertainment ranging from film through to dance, taking in comedy and children's events along the way. It is also the venue for the annual Newbury pantomime (oh yes it is!).

Newbury also has the Watermill Theatre (01635 46044), a professional theatre company offering eight or nine new shows a year. The company here was recently described in a national newspaper as in 'the premier league of British regional theatres.'

Newbury also hosts an annual Spring Festival for a fortnight in the middle of May, featuring international musicians and music covering the spectrum from opera to jazz along with visual arts.

Finally in Newbury, the Desmoulin Gallery (01635 35001), situated in an old granary on the wharf, shows a changing collection of art, both local and regional, and is worth repeat visits.

When it comes to recreation of a more physical kind, there are a few options. The Kennet Leisure Centre in Thatcham (01635 871112) has a 25m indoor swimming pool with beach area and spa pool as well as a flume and occasional inflatable sessions. This comprehensive centre also has a fitness gym, sports hall and dance studio. Also around Thatcham is the Newbury Leisure Park which includes the Lakeside Superbowl (01635 874222) amongst its attractions.

The Northcroft Leisure Centre in Newbury (01635 31199) has a 25m indoor pool and 70m outdoor summer pool as well as a sports hall and health suite. A smaller facility shared with the Downs School in Compton in Newbury is the Downland Sports Centre (01635 578866) which has a gym and sports hall designed to serve the local community.

Perhaps Newbury's most significant entertainment attraction is its racecourse, one of the country's leading horse racing venues, staging around thirty days racing a year, both on the flat and over the sticks, including the world-famous Hennessey Cognac Gold Cup. The racecourse was recently refurbished and is also used as a conference and exhibition centre and has not only a golf course but also a fitness centre with swimming pool and gymnasium.

When it comes to night-time entertainment, Newbury is again the place to head, although there is regular live music at the Kings Head in Thatcham (01635 862145) and the Newbury Leisure Park has the nightclub Venom (01635 878222).

Newbury has its own night club in Liquid (01635 237144) and live music can also be heard at the Donnington Valley Hotel (01635 551199), with jazz at the Newbury Jazz Platform at the Northcroft Sports Centre on the second Friday of each month and at the Hilton Hotel in Newbury (01635 43405).

Newbury Market Cross.

SECTION D   CROFTON TO DEVIZES

This page, top, and opposite above: *Devizes Wharf.*
Above left: *Pewsey – King Alfred's statue.*
Above right: *Devizes Market Place.*

Opposite below: *Devizes Corn Exchange.*

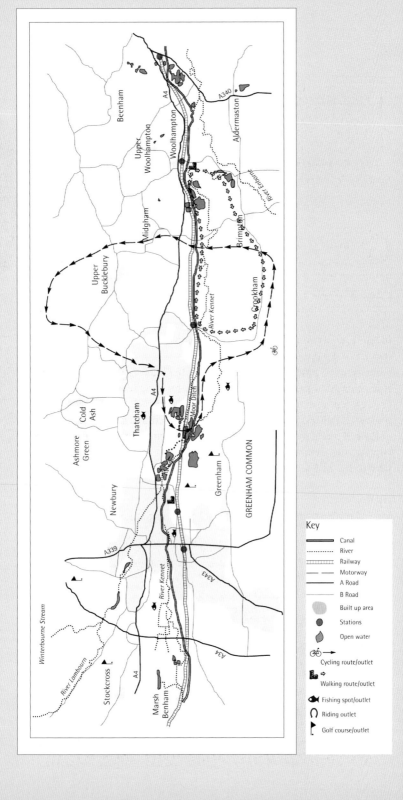

Key

▬▬▬▬	Canal
··········	River
▦▦▦▦	Railway
– – – –	Motorway
———	A Road
———	B Road
▨	Built up area
⬤	Stations
⬟	Open water
🚲→	Cycling route/outlet
👢⇨	Walking route/outlet
🐟	Fishing spot/outlet
∩	Riding outlet
▶	Golf course/outlet

SAMPLING

INTRODUCTION

There is plenty of countryside to enjoy in between the two main towns in this section. South of Newbury the (in)famous Greenham Common, along with the Newbury Racecourse dominate the landscape, while the Kennet Valley continues to etch a wide furrow running east to west.

The OS Explorer Maps covering this stretch are No.159, Reading and No.158, Newbury and Hungerford.

WALKING

Greenham Common, restored from its notorious role as a military site, now has a number of marked paths cutting across it. A unique feature of these walks is the opportunity to take in old bomb-sites and even a cruise missile silo enclosure! Given its history, it seems all the more remarkable to consider that the common is also a designated Site of Special Scientific Interest (SSSI). Mention was made in the last section of the Bowdown Woods Nature Reserve, between these two commons.

Snelsmore Common Country Park, off the Wantage Road in Newbury, is another SSSI and is an important area for ground-nesting birds such as nightjars and woodlarks. Finally, Newbury has plans to establish a town trail, taking the walker past a series of commissioned sculptures.

Walk B starts by walking away from the canal and up alongside the edge of the Kennet Valley before descending again to join the canal near to the turf-side Monkey Marsh Lock.

SECTION B WALK
From Woolhampton Lock and Back via Brimpton and Croockham

Description:	*A combination of field and road walking looking down into the Kennet Valley with some noticeable gradients.*
Distance:	*6¼ miles*
Duration:	*2½hrs*
Staring point:	*Grid Reference 572665, OS Explorer 158*
Nearest refreshment:	*The Travellers Friend, Crookham*

Start from the Row Barge car park, turning right and up the road away from the canal. On reaching the second footpath on the right by a metal gate, head west along a track, with a disused gravel pit soon becoming visible on the right. Where another path joins from the right strike out half left, sticking with the track aiming for the church spire in front of you. When the

SECTION D   CROFTON TO DEVIZES

Top: *Moored boats at Honey Street.*
Above: *Golden Swan, Wilcot.*

Opposite above, left and right: *The Waterfront Inn, Pewsey.*
Opposite below: *A signwriter's boat at Pewsey Wharf.*

track curves to the right pick up the path straight in front of you through trees.

On reaching a road turn right, passing a shop on your right and the church on your left. Stay with the road as it climbs gently upwards, past Brimpton village hall, and a half thatched, half tiled cottage on your left. The road levels out and passes through Crookham. Manor Farm here is worth noting for its Georgian architecture.

Enter or pass, as is your preference, The Traveller's Friend and continue past a caravan park and at a crossroads with a public bridleway turn right by a bus stop. Follow this down to and past Highfield Farm, after which the path loses its metalled surface and becomes more of a track. This passes by some woodland and soon drops quite steeply, eventually flattening out near a farm.

Leave the track and go straight ahead through a gate, bearing left to pick up a road. Pass a football ground to your left and you will come out onto a road, the Kennet River and canal on your right. The turf-sided Monkey Marsh Lock is to your back and worth looking at, otherwise head east back towards Woolhampton following the towpath. Light industrial canalside development gives way to a more pleasing vista, with the towpath crossing over at the Cranwell Bridge and back over Oxlease Bridge.

Walking equipment outlets along this section include:
- Millets, Newbury (01635 40070)
- X5, Newbury (01635 237666)

CYCLING

The steep sides of the Kennet Valley, along with the relative paucity of good paths, can make designing a route for this section a challenge. That said, there is little option but to turn the gradients to your advantage and catch some views. Our recommended route starts at the car park at Crookham Common near Crookham House and heads east past the caravan park before picking up the bridleway on the left after Manor Farm.

Follow this down to the road and bear left again, passing over both the river and then the canal. Cross over the A4 and head up a minor road, through Midgham, and pick up the footpath on the left shortly after Midgham Park Farm. This brings you to Bucklebery Common where you head left (west) and through Upper Bucklebery. Stick with this road as it climbs until you reach Lawrence Lane where you turn left.

This then heads downhill into Thatcham. On reaching a T-junction, turn right and left at the next, which brings you back to the A4 where you turn right and take the immediate next left turning. Follow this round (you are now on National Cycle Route 4), picking up the bridleway on the left which brings you past the Jubilee Lake and then along the south of the Long Lake. Head left on reaching a junction of paths and, on reaching the towpath, head east (left) as far as Long Cut Swing Bridge (No.44).

Head over the bridge and follow this path uphill until you reach a road where you turn left. This bends left shortly afterwards and you need to pick up a track heading right which rejoins the road, which in turn takes you back to your starting point, a total of around 14 miles.

Cycle outlets along this section include:
- Banjo Cycles, Newbury (01635 43186)
- The Cycle Shop, Newbury (01635 582100)
- M.J Muttram, Thatcham (01635 868740)

RIDING

Buckleberry Common is good for short rides in this section, and there are a number of bridleways including one that links Upper Buckleberry with Colthrop and various others south of the canal, most of which head up into the hills. There is a further path heading due north out of Newbury which eventually links up with Curridge.

Horse-riding establishments and outlets along this section include:
- Maple Ash Livery Stables, Newbury (01635 247094)

FISHING

The Thatcham (01635 860804) and Newbury (01635 43394) Angling Associations control most of the waters along this stretch, with the former probably the most significant player (see 'Learn More and Links' for website addresses).

Waters controlled by the Thatcham AA include a stretch of the Kennet near the railway station which offers both good barbel as well as the occasional carp, roach and dace. The association also controls the complex of three lakes round the Discovery Centre comprising Jubilee and Long Lakes and Horderns-mere.

The first of these produces carp around the 20lb mark, bream to double figures and tench to over 7lb, as well as some large pike and a variety of other fish. Even larger carp and tench can be found at Long Lake, along with roach, perch and pike. Horderns-mere is probably the most picturesque of the lakes and also the smallest, and is a good spot for roach, rudd, tench, bream, perch, pike and carp.

The association controls the section between Thatcham and Widmead Lock as well as the Whitehouse stretch of the canal to the west of Newbury. This stretch offers a variety of fish including chub over 5lb, bream to 4lb and perch around 2lb. Some care needs to be taken fishing the canal around this section as in parts it has been over-run by crayfish. Newbury AA controls the stretch between Bulls Lock and Ham Lock and between Greenham Lock and Greenham Island as well as Northcroft to Guyers Bridge.

SECTION E   DEVIZES TO AVONCLIFF

Top: *Avoncliff Aqueduct.*
Above: *Bradford on Avon Bridge.*

Opposite top: *Bradford on Avon Wharf.*
Opposite middle: *Caen Hill from the top.*
Opposite below: *Bikes for hire at Bradford on Avon.*

A number of other associations also operate small sections of the canal along this stretch. The Civil Service Angling Association (see 'Learn More and Links') also controls 3½ miles of the Middle Kennet around Newbury at Ham Bridge (No.50) which offers both coarse and fly fishing. Incidentally, trout are also available at the Newbury Trout Farm (0789 9905544) where rainbows as large as 20lb have been fished, as well as browns, and at Frobury Farm (01635 298436) which offers the chance to fish for rainbows.

The RDAA controls the stretch of the canal between Heales Lock and Midgham Bridge whilst the stretch between Whitehouse and Greenham Lock is controlled by Twickenham PS. The Reed Thatcham AA controls the junction with the Kennet at Northcroft and two stretches at Midgham Lock.

Outlets selling fishing supplies along this stretch include:

- Crownmead Angling Centre (01635 863092)
- Field & Stream, Newbury (01635 43186)
- Thatcham Angling Centre (01635 871450)

OTHER

Newbury is particularly well endowed with golf courses which offer a good opportunity to sample the surrounding countryside. The main courses are:

- Deanwood Park Golf Club, Newbury (01635 48772) – *9 holes, 2,114 yards*
- Donnington Valley Golf Club, Newbury (01635 568140) – *18 holes, 6,353 yards*
- Newbury Racecourse Golf Course (01635 551464) – *18 holes, 6,500 yards, a challenging flat links course with a twenty bay driving range*
- Newbury and Crookham Golf Club (01635 40035) – *18 holes, 5,940 yards*

SECTION C
MARSH BENHAM TO CROFTON

SECTION E   DEVIZES TO AVONCLIFF

Above: *Sells Green from a bridge.*

Opposite top: *The River Avon from Avoncliff Aqueduct.*
Opposite middle: *Hilperton, The Knap.*
Opposite below: *The Barge Inn, Seend.*

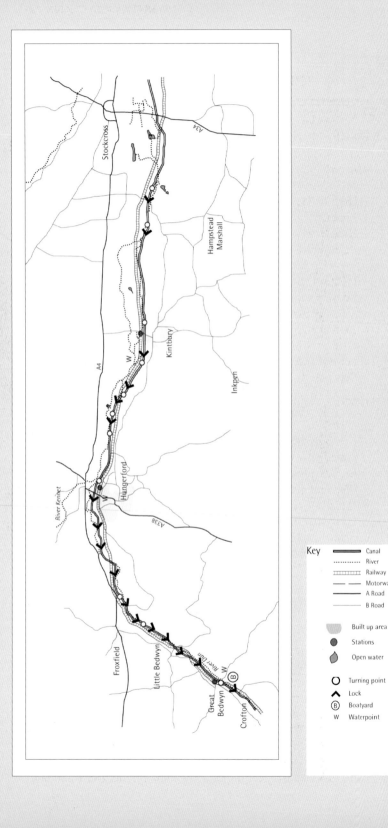

Key

- Canal
- .... River
- ┼┼┼┼┼┼ Railway
- – – – Motorway
- A Road
- B Road

▨ Built up area

● Stations

◗ Open water

○ Turning point

⌄ Lock

Ⓑ Boatyard

W Waterpoint

Stockcross

Hampstead Marshall

A34

A4

W

Kintbury

Inkpen

River Kennet

Hungerford

A338

Froxfield

Little Bedwyn

River Dun

Great Bedwyn

W

Ⓑ

Crofton

SHAPERS

THE CANAL ON THIS STRETCH

KEY FACTS

LENGTH: 13 miles

BOATYARDS: 1

Bedwyn Boat Services

WATERPOINTS: 3

Kintbury
Hungerford
Bedwyn Wharf

TURNING POINTS: 11

Dreweat's Bridge	Hungerford Town Bridge
Kintbury Station	Oakhill Farm
Kintbury Vicarage	Oakhill Down
Wire Lock Bridge	Fore Bridge
Lower Denford	Great Bedwyn Wharf
Dun Mill	

LOCKS: 17

Copse Lock (6ft)	Froxfield Bottom Lock (7ft)
Dreweat's Lock (5ft 9in)	
Kintbury Lock (5ft 9in)	Froxfield Middle Lock (6ft 11in)
Brunsden Lock (4ft 11in)	
Wire Lock (6ft 10in)	Oakhill Down Lock (5ft 11in)
Dunmill Lock (5ft 8in)	
Hungerford Lock (8ft)	Little Bedwyn Lock (6ft 11in)
Hungerford Marsh Lock (8ft 1in)	Potter's Lock (7ft 6in)
Cobbler's Lock (81ft 3in)	Burnt Mill Lock (7ft 9in)
Picketfield Lock (7ft)	Bedwyn Church Lock (7ft 11in)

The canal now sinks into a comforting rurality, with the pretty village of Kintbury and the ancient market town of Hungerford offering the only distractions before the Bedwyns. The locks continue to come on thick and fast, with the canal itself taking a determined southward path after Hungerford and the climb towards the canal's summit.

After the wide water leading up to Hamstead, the aptly named Copse Lock sits in a shady arbour, and on emerging from the trees the rural landscape continues with more fields and woodlands

SECTION F   AVONCLIFF TO BATH

This page, top: *Bath Abbey.*
This page, bottom: *The Roman Baths at Bath.*

Opposite top: *A typical Bath arch.*
Opposite middle: *The Roman Baths exterior.*
Opposite bottom: *Bath bridges.*

to the left with the river, never far away, sitting in a valley on the right.

A tributary of this now makes Dreweat's Lock a challenge with a sluice and weir just the other side, after which canal and towpath head to a small wood for sanctuary. Look out for excellent views to the left at the lock.

Kintbury Lock has temporary mooring posts before it which are often occupied by large horse-drawn trip boats. The lock itself sits beside the station, the railway having come alongside, with the Dundas Arms pub, re-

> The Kintbury Horse Boat Co. runs out from Kintbury and offers day trips (01488 658866).

nowned for its food, on the other side adjacent to the Kennet. A good run of visitor moorings follows with a water point early on as well as a sanitary station. Kintbury is a worthwhile stop, with three pubs spaced well apart and a village store up the hill, and a pretty church near the canal.

Immediately after the moorings at the aptly named Vicarage Bridge, the canal widens out in front of the Old Vicarage. A straight stretch follows with more informal moorings. This is a very pleasant part of the canal with the towpath still to the right, although by the standards of this waterway it becomes less defined and narrower along here.

Between Brunsden and Wire Locks the railway crosses the towpath, followed by a turning point at the attractive Dunmill Lock shortly after, where a finger-sign directs lock operators to cross over the bridge. The theme of regular locks, so familiar before Newbury, is now firmly re-established with barely a mile going by without at least one. Dunmill itself

> St Lawrence's in Hungerford was built in the early nineteenth century of Bath stone, the transport of which represented the first commercial cargo on the canal.

looms like a vanishing point after a long curve in the water and once again there are views of the river to the right of the towpath.

Hungerford church now pierces the skyline briefly to announce the imminent arrival of that town, although it soon disappears behind the high hedge accompanying the towpath along this stretch. There are mooring opportunities here, with a line of birch trees obscuring the town so that it comes as something of a surprise when it finally appears. There are formal moorings here and all the shops you would expect from a small market town.

The town is passed through quickly and after Hungerford Lock and Swing Bridge the scenery is mainly marsh and scrub, although this is not unattractive, especially in the long run up to Marsh Lock which sits in the middle of Freeman's Marsh, a Site of Special Scientific Interest. Rather inconveniently, Marsh Lock has a swing bridge right across its middle. The views here are wide and the towpath can become a little bumpy.

After Cobblers Lock the other side of the marsh, complete with a pretty lock-side cottage, the canal uses an aqueduct to cross the river which spreads out below to the left. As if not to be outdone, the railway crosses both and heads off to the right. This is another pretty stretch with tree plantations and the hidden River Dun on the non-towpath side and open fields to the left.

Bedwyn is home to the unique Stone Museum with examples of the work of seven generations of stonemasons in the village.

Before long the spire of Little Bedwyn church heralds the arrival of that village, with its pair of footbridges over the railway and canal. There are fields and farmland to the left and two more locks before arriving at Great Bedwyn, which is separated from the canal by meadows, on the other side of which sits the busy railway station and the main part of the village. There are good moorings here before the bridge and a water and sanitary point, as well as a car park after it.

PRINCIPAL TOWNS AND VILLAGES ALONG THIS STRETCH

CROFTON
A scattering of houses north-east of the nearby pumping station.

FROXFIELD
A small hamlet overshadowed by the fact that the A4 passes to one side of it and by the imposing presence of spectacular Somerset Hospital on its eastern edge.

GREAT BEDWYN
The river, canal and railway all coincide at the foot of the hill on which Great Bedwyn sits. A surprising village, Great Bedwyn is also the gateway to the Crofton Pumping Station.

HAMPSTEAD MARSHALL
A small village which also has a Dogs Trust Rehoming Centre and the Elm Farm Research Centre.

The otherwise quiet town of Hungerford is perhaps known to many for the Hungerford Massacre when local man Michael Ryan shot sixteen people dead in 1987 before killing himself.

HUNGERFORD
Hungerford's picturesque wharf alone makes this a place worth pausing in, even if you do not need to avail yourself of the rare opportunity on this stretch to top up with supplies. An historic town with much to offer those who linger, Hungerford sits mainly to the south of the canal, rising up on a gentle hill.

INKPEN
Inkpen sits on top of a hill and comprises three parts, Upper and Lower Inkpen, as well as Inkpen Common. The former hosts an industrial estate

SECTION F   AVONCLIFF TO BATH

This page, top: *Pulteney Bridge and the weir at Bath.*
This page, bottom: *Bath's Paradise Gardens.*

Opposite top: *A Bath side street.*
Opposite bottom: *Bath's Royal Circus.*

and consequently some more modern housing, whilst Lower Inkpen has a certain air of exclusivity and the Common defines the eastern limit.

KINTBURY

A village of many parts with a 1930s estate of semi-detached houses sitting side by side with thatched cottages and more modern housing. The canal and railway sit at the bottom of a hill, where there is also an attractive mill building.

LITTLE BEDWYN

Hiding itself behind a large brick wall south of the canal, Little Bedwyn is slightly less shy to the north where there is the church and a charming collection of period cottages, as well as the railway line.

HISTORY

As the canal drifts away from the 'new town' of Newbury and away from the influence of Reading and its Abbey, so the towns and villages in this section might be expected to have a quieter history, independent of wider affairs of state. To an extent this is true, but the influence of lords and kings still prevails in the places featured here, with Hungerford and the smaller Hampstead Marshall standing out.

Hungerford has claims to have been the most significant town along this stretch for the longest period of time, although it only really came into prominence in the dark ages. Prior to this, the Romans seemed to favour Kintbury, where a large fourth-century bathhouse has been excavated west of the village.

Hungerford's name is thought to derive from the Danish King Hingwar, also known, somewhat intriguingly, as Ivarr the Boneless. One of Hingwar's claims to fame is being the man who shot St Edmund, who also acted as King of East Anglia, in 869. Hingwar himself died at Hungerford, probably by drowning, on his way to meet the Saxons in battle at Ethandun. This battle was to mark the end of the Dane's rule in the south of England.

The Saxons were also active in Kintbury, its name being thought to derive from the Saxon for 'Fort on the River Kennet'. Saxon pits have been also been discovered

Ethandun is thought by some to be the modern Eddington north of Hungerford, although stronger claims can be made for Edington in Wiltshire.

near the village. There is some suggestion that these may mark the site of a Holy place revered by the Saxons, not least Thegn Wulfgar, the owner of Inkpen in 931, who left his village to the owners of an unspecified Holy Place at 'Kentbury'. Great Bedwyn also featured significantly around this time, with some evidence that it was the site of an earthwork fortification known as Chisbury castle. The village was also the location of a bitter battle between the kings of Mercia and Wessex in 695.

Like Newbury, Kintbury was earmarked as a new town by the Normans and given the rights to hold a weekly market and two three-day fairs. Although initially successful, the village was fairly quickly overtaken by Hungerford, which grew rapidly. Indeed, the medieval street plan set out here in the twelfth century remains largely intact today.

It is around this time that some of the other villages along here began to develop. By the eleventh century, Great Bedwyn was a borough with twenty-five burbages and even a mint, and the church dates back a century earlier. Froxfield also had its own church by the twelfth century, as did Kintbury.

Although relatively unprepossessing these days, in the twelfth century Hampstead Marshall was a more significant place. The bumps still visible around the church mark a deserted medieval village, and possibly a castle. Local landlord, John Marshall, whose family gave their name to the village, was a man of some substance, close to the Empress Matilda, and the pair of them were besieged at Newbury Castle in 1253. The siege only ended when Marshall gave up his seven-year-old son William as a hostage for his future good behaviour. In time, Hampstead Marshall was to welcome much friendlier kings. Henry III was entertained there in 1218 and in the 1350s Edward III liked to spend Christmas in the village,

> William Marshall grew up to become both Earl of Pembroke and Protector of England. He made his home at Hampstead Marshall his primary residence, owned Newbury and defeated the French in battle.

not least because he enjoyed the local hunting. By this time the estate had passed into royal hands.

Another place with royal connections was Hungerford, or to give it its full title by the thirteenth century, Hungerford Regis, although it was around this time that ownership passed from the King to the Dukes of Lancaster. This led to the town's association with John O'Gaunt, a man whose memory is revered in the town, for it was he who granted fishing rights in the Kennet to the local townspeople. These rights subsided over the following centuries and the town tried to have them revived under Elizabeth. A lengthy court case was only resolved when the Queen herself intervened and ruled in favour of the town. To this day the town still celebrates Hocktide the second Tuesday after Easter, in gratitude.

The oldest building in Hungerford is The Bear Inn, which operated as a hospice in 1464 and was visited by Elizabeth, whose coachman died there. The Bear also played host to King Charles I for three days during the Civil War and the future King William III was staying there when the Royal Commissioners arrived and offered him the crown.

As with other towns along the eastern half of the Kennet & Avon Canal, the Bath Road proved to be commercially important, although less so than elsewhere, with many of the villages lying far enough to the south of the road to be unaffected by it. Great Bedwyn managed to have so many alehouses in 1648 that neighbouring parishes regarded the place as a descending into disrepute – and it wasn't even on the road!

The coming of the canal itself, however, was a different matter. In the last decade of the eighteenth century, Kintbury, in particular, was inundated with navvies cutting the canal, which may go some way to explaining the large number of pubs in the town.

Agriculture remained the economic mainstay, with Great Bedwyn having a population of just over 2,000 in 1831, two thirds of which worked the land. It was around this time, of course, that the Swing Riots took place, with Kintbury at the centre of the action as the place where the whole uprising was put down, somewhat bloodily.

These days, the villages along this stretch are much quieter and a pleasure to visit.

THE NATURAL LANDSCAPE

The rivers Dun and Kennet meet at Hungerford, with the former accompanying the canal to the west and the latter to the east, their respective valleys forming a natural conduit for the artificial waterway. The Kennet's floor becomes narrower along this section, emphasising the climb on both sides of the towpath.

East of Hungerford the canal is accompanied by a patchwork of woodland, although after passing through the town this immediately gives way to the occasionally windswept open ground of Hungerford Common. After Freeman's Marsh the valley floor becomes even more constrictive, although there are still views to be had, with woodland to the south-east providing good walking territory.

ACCESS AND TRANSPORT

ROADS

The A4 remains the near constant companion to the canal along this section, passing just north of the towpath all the way through Hungerford, diverging only when it reaches Froxfield. The A338 passes north–south through Hungerford and provides a link to the network of B roads south of the canal, including the Hungerford Road which links that town to Kintbury and follows a path parallel to the towpath to the south. Generally speaking, the area to the north of the canal is much less densely populated with both towns and roads.

RAIL

Hungerford, Great Bedwyn and Kintbury each have railway stations, with services operated by First Great Western Link (08457 484950). Both Great Bedwyn and Kintbury sit right by the canal, whilst the station at Hungerford is also close at hand.

For more detailed information contact National Train Enquiries on 08457 484950 or www.nationalrail.co.uk.

BUSES

The following list sets out the main bus services on this section, although it is advisable to check before using them as some buses only run on certain days and others may have been withdrawn since publication of this Guide. It is also worth checking for more local services.

- 13 – *Hungerford to Newbury via Inkpen and Kintbury (Reading Buses)*
- 20 – *Hungerford/Bedwyn to Marlborough/Pewsey. Services vary (W&D)*
- 20A – *Hungerford to Marlborough via Froxfield, Great Bedwyn and Bedwyn (W&D)*
- 23 – *Hungerford to Marlborough via Great Bedwyn (Barnes Coaches)*
- 221 – *Great Bedwyn to Pewsey. Tuesday only (Tourist Coaches)*
- 222 – *Marlborough to Pewsey via Great Bedwyn and Hungerford. Thursday only (Tourist)*
- H1 – *Hungerford circular local service (Weavaway)*
- WB4 – *Devizes to Pewsey via Great Bedwyn. Saturdays only (Hatts Coaches)*
- X2 – *Marlborough to Newbury via Froxfield and Hungerford. Saturday only (W&D)*
- X20 – *Hungerford to Marlborough. Saturday only (W&D)*

In addition, the National Express coach service 402 links Trowbridge, Melksham, Devizes, Hungerford and Newbury on its way into London once every day of the week, passing through a number of the sections covered in this Guide.

Contact details for bus operators in this area are listed below, although Traveline (www.traveline.org.uk) on 0870 6082608 can give details of specific services between 7 a.m. and 10 p.m.:

- Barnes Coaches, Aldbourne (01672 540330)
- Hatts Coaches, Chippenham (01249 740444)
- National Express, Birmingham (08705 808080)
- Reading Buses, Reading (0118 9594000)
- Tourist Coaches, Salisbury (01722 338359)
- Weavaway, Newbury (01635 820028)
- W&D – Wilts and Dorset Bus Company, Poole (01202 678291)

TAXIS

The following list gives a selection of the taxi operators in this section:
- 0800 Cars, Hungerford (01488 686164)
- Taff's Taxis, Hungerford (01488 685380)
- Hungerford Cars, Hungerford (01488 685467)

SECTION C

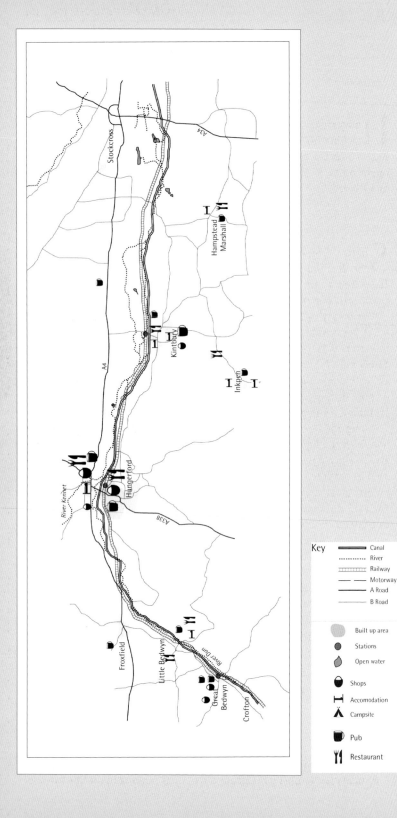

Key

Canal
River
Railway
Motorway
A Road
B Road

Built up area
Stations
Open water
Shops
Accomodation
Campsite
Pub
Restaurant

BASICS

INTRODUCTION

Hungerford, in the middle of this section, is the main location for picking up basic supplies, although the surrounding villages also host a number of good pubs. Great Bedwyn marks the last canalside opportunity to stock up before the long lockless pound between here and Devizes.

SHOPPING

Shops in Hungerford fall into two districts, with the canal acting at the dividing line. To the north lies the historic Bear at Hungerford Hotel and a run of charity and antique shops as well as some more traditional outlets along the A4 to the north.

The area to the south, running uphill alongside the A338 is more what you would expect in such a town, although charity shops remain a feature. A large Somerfield supermarket is hidden away off the High Street and there is a Co-op on the main drag itself, alongside the usual collection of banks, building societies, off-licences and pharmacies – most of the places, in fact, you would need for a supplies stock up, including some good old-style bakers and butchers.

Alongside these one or two curiosities stand out, including a kitchen specialist, a shop selling furniture made out of railway sleepers and a creative toy shop, as well as a small arcade selling yet more antiques. As well as these there is also a Costcutter on the edge of town.

For those with wheeled transport, Highclose Farm Shop (01488 686770) on the A4 out of Hungerford is well worth a visit. Here there is a cheese counter, coffee shop, organic meat counter, bakery and deli as well as fruit and vegetables, including pick your own in season. Also worth a detour is the Farleigh Natural Springs Trout Farm (01225 762059) which sells fresh and smoked trout.

Kintbury has its Corner Stores at the top of the hill, incorporating an off-licence. Along the way there is a small collection of shops including a baker and a fishmonger as well as the High Street Pottery (01488 657388).

Otherwise, Froxfield also offers antiques and Great Bedwyn has a bakery in Church Street along with an incredible post office and general store, remarkable less for its contents (which are fairly limited) than for its exterior, which is made up of funeral memorials from the adjacent Stone Museum.

EATING AND DRINKING

There is a fair selection of drinking holes along this stretch, with many (although by no means all) of them moving in the 'gastro-pub' direction, so be prepared to open your wallet. Kintbury and Hungerford both have a good selection of pubs, while Inkpen and Great Bedwyn are also worth a visit.

- The White Hart, Hampstead Marshall (01488 658201) – *also a restaurant*
- The Blue Ball, Kintbury (01488 608126) – *up the hill*
- The Dundas Arms Hotel, Kintbury (01488 658263) – *on the canal*
- The Prince of Wales, Kintbury (01488 658269) – *up the hill*
- The Swan Inn, Lower Inkpen (01488 668326) – *includes the Cygnet restaurant*
- The Crown and Garter, Inkpen (01488 668325)
- The Bear, Hungerford (01488 682512)
- Borough Arms, Hungerford (01488 683233)
- Downgate Down View, Hungerford (01488682708)

– east of Station Road footbridge
- The John O'Gaunt Inn, Hungerford (01488 683535)
- The Lamb, Hungerford (01488 71552)
- The Plume of Feathers, Hungerford (01488 682154)
- The Railway Tavern, Hungerford (01488 683100)
- The Sun Inn, Hungerford (01488 682162)
- The Pelican Inn, Froxfield (01488 682479)
- The Harrow, Little Bedwyn (01672 870871) – *a fine dining restaurant with a renowned wine list*
- The Cross Keys, Great Bedwyn (01672 870678)
- The Three Tuns, Great Bedwyn (01672 870280)

As already remarked upon, many of the pubs double up as restaurants, whilst the hotels listed below do likewise. A selection of other eateries along this stretch includes:

- Bistro Roque (01488 658398) – *on the Kintbury to Inkpen road*
- Azura, Hungerford (01488 644643) – *coffee and sandwiches*
- Café Delice, Hungerford (01488 686700)
- Casanova, Hungerford (01488 682588) – *Italian*
- Hungerford Gourmet

Oriental Food Takeaway, Hungerford (01488 686898) – *Chinese*
- The Number Five Bar and Restaurant, Hungerford (01488 686390) – *wine bar*
- The Tutti Pole, Hungerford (01488 682515) – *tea shop near the canal*

The Kennet & Avon Trust also has a café at their regional headquarters at the Crofton Pumping Station (01672 870300).

SLEEPING

Hotels tend towards the upper end of the range along this section, although there is the occasional smaller family-run establishment. In addition, there is a reasonable selection of guest houses, although campers will be disappointed.

HOTELS

- Dundas Arms Hotel, Kintbury (01488 658263) – *canalside, five rooms*
- The Bear at Hungerford (01488 682512) – *recently refurbished historic hotel*
- Littlecote House Hotel, Hungerford (01488 682509) – *Grade I Tudor mansion*
- Marshgate Cottage Hotel, Hungerford (01488 682307) – *small family-run hotel overlooking the canal*
- The Three Swans Hotel, Hungerford (01488 682721) – *independent hotel with fifteen rooms*
- The Pelican Inn, Froxfield (01488 682479)

BED AND BREAKFAST/GUEST HOUSES

- Holtwood Gate, Hamstead Marshall (01635 253454)
- Holy Lodge, Kintbury (01488 668244)
- Beacon House, Inkpen (01488 668640)
- The Crown and Garter, Inkpen (01488 668325)
- Anne's B&B, Hungerford (01488 682290)
- Culdrose, Hungerford (01488 682583)
- Plough House, Hungerford (01488 686008)
- Wilton House, Hungerford (01488 684228)
- Bridge Cottage, Little Bedwyn (01672 870795)

CAMPING
There are no camping sites or camping equipment stores along this section.

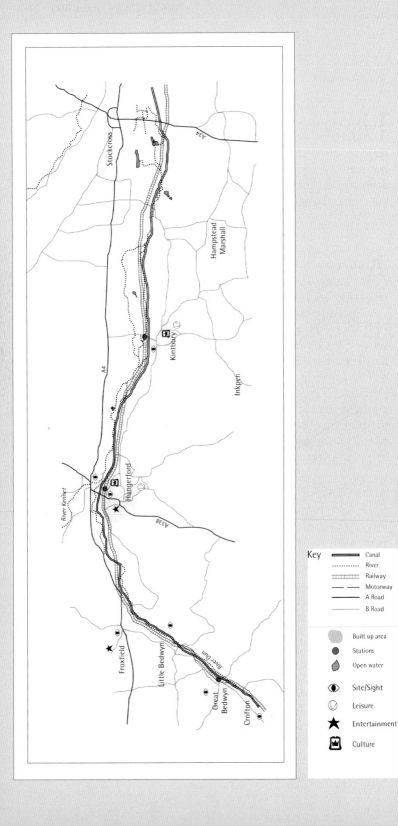

Key

━━━━	Canal
··········	River
▦▦▦▦	Railway
━ ━ ━	Motorway
━━━	A Road
───	B Road

⬤	Built up area
●	Stations
◗	Open water
◉	Site/Sight
◔	Leisure
★	Entertainment
⬔	Culture

Stockcross

A34

Hampstead Marshall

Kintbury

Inkpen

A4

River Kennet

Hungerford

A338

Froxfield

Little Bedwyn

River Dun

Great Bedwyn

Crofton

SEEING AND DOING

INTRODUCTION

Hungerford is the main town along this stretch although Kintbury and Great Bedwyn at either end are also worth a visit. In between there are many smaller communities and a lot of farmland. The canal continues its east–west trajectory as far as Hungerford where it suddenly plunges south towards its summit marked by the tall chimney of the Crofton Pumping Station.

SIGHTS

Although not open to the public, the Elm Farm Research Centre in Hampstead Marshall is interesting as a farm dedicated to the research of organic and sustainable farming methods.

Kintbury, by the canal, is a popular summer spot, although the noise from the trains can take something away from the sense of quiet and solitude. Look down to the east and you may be lucky enough to spot the Kennet Horse Boat (01488 658866), one of the few remaining horse-drawn canal boat trips.

Kintbury's imposing church of St Mary, perhaps best viewed from the other side of the canal was a Saxon Minster, although most of the current building is twelfth century. Inside you will see a number of noteworthy monuments and a painted text remembering 'Wild Will Darell' of Littlecote House who murdered a baby born in his house by throwing it into a blazing fire. Expected to hang, he escaped this fate by giving his estate to the judge, who was also his cousin.

> The Bear is known to have been a hospice as early as 1464 and may have been connected with the Hospital of St John.

Hungerford Wharf, in the heart of that town, is very picturesque and acts as something of a focal point, dividing the town into two parts. The Rose of Hungerford trip boat (01488 683389) can often be seen moored up here. Look out also for the wisteria-draped Bridge Cottage.

North of the canal the most impressive building is probably The Bear Hotel where the River Dun flows on the opposite side of the road. To the south it is worth wandering along the High Street as Hungerford is unusual in having retained its medieval street plan; the houses here have long narrow strips of land trailing perpendicularly backwards. Towards the top there is also an imposing Victorian red-brick Town Hall with Byzantine-style tower.

> Hungerford's Town Crier is known as the Bellman and he wanders about the town in a uniform of hunting pink with a black silk laced hat, making various pronouncements. He is very approachable and will give information on the town if asked.

SECTION C

The building that stands out the most, however, is the church of St Lawrence. Not that old, it dates from 1816 and was built on the site of a Norman church to a Georgian Gothic style. The church has an oak-panelled ceiling and some impressive stained-glass windows, including three dedicated to Revd Anstice, vicar from 1866 to 1894, when all the windows were replaced. The west tower has an embattled parapet with angled pinnacles and has a peal of eight bells as well as a Sanctus bell.

Hungerford retains a ceremony known as 'Tutti Day' or 'Hocktide', held the second Tuesday after Easter. This marks the end of the financial and administrative year when all the Commissioners to the Court are summoned by the Town Crier while two Tutti Men wander around the town visiting each house with Common rights (around 100 altogether). The Tutti Men used to collect a penny from each householder but these days are given a kiss from the lady of the house and receive an orange in return.

Hungerford's other main feature is its Common, 200 acres of open parkland on the edge of the town which is still used for grazing cattle as can be seen by the 'Down Gate' to stop them entering the town. The Hungerford Marsh Swing Bridge sits in the centre of the Common and can be a difficult obstacle for boaters on a wet and windy day.

Further to the west it is impossible to miss the vast Somerset Hospital in Froxfield. Founded in 1694 for 'twenty clergy and thirty lay widows' by Sarah, Duchess Dowager of Somerset, this quadrangle of fifty almshouses dominates the approach to the village. The building is fronted by an impressive archway added in 1813 and the visitor who passes through it is presented with a view of immaculate lawns and well-kept borders with a small parish church in the centre.

> Froxfield locals claim that on moonlit nights it is possible to see the ghost of the baby burner Will Darrell being chased by the Hounds of Hell. Darrell came to a sticky end eventually when he broke his neck jumping over a stile.

Little Bedwyn is a pretty spot, with its footbridge and eighteenth- and nineteenth-century buildings, as well as the River Dun, but it is somewhat overshadowed by the larger Great Bedwyn. There are two buildings of note here, St Mary's church and the Stone Museum. The church dates back to 1092 and has a memorial to John Seymour, father of the ill-fated Jane Seymour, along with another to the Duke of Somerset. The oldest parts of the building are the piers and arches of the nave, which are in transition Norman style combined with early English ornament.

The Stone Museum in Great Bedwyn, over the road and adjacent to the village store, is something of a curiosity with stone memorials lining the side and embedded into the brickwork. The Lloyd family have been stonemasons in the yard here for over 200 years and the museum is a testament to the mason's art, including a number of unusual edifices such as one for a Battle of Britain pilot.

Finally in this section is the significant, for the canal at least, attraction of the Crofton Pumping Station (01672 870300) with its unmissable chimney. The pumping station was built in 1807 to bring water up to the summit of the canal and, during pumping days, the old steam engines installed nearly 200 years ago continue to do the job they were installed for, with the electrical replacements that normally top the canal up being temporarily switched off.

The engines in question are an 1812 Boulton & Watt and an 1846 Harvey & Hayle beam engine, the latter, a Sims Combined Cylinders Engine, having been the replacement for another Boulton & Watt engine installed in 1809. Visitors are also treated to the sight of a number of small stationary steam engines in the boiler house which also function during steam days.

> The summit of the Kennet & Avon sits between Crofton and Burbage and is 450ft above sea level and 40ft higher than any reliable local water source, hence the need for some kind of device to keep the canal topped up.

CULTURE AND ENTERTAINMENT

Newbury acts as the main source of cultural sustenance in this part of West Berkshire and East Wiltshire (see Section B), although this is not to suggest that Hungerford is a cultural desert. The town hosts a three-week festival every July known as the Hungerford and District Community Arts Festival or HADCAF (01488 684901) with a variety of arts and leisure events and entertainments, and an accent of making as much as possible free to attend. As such, features of the festival range from guided walks to open gardens, literature, poetry, film and music shows.

Kintbury also stages regular amateur dramatics through the year in the local Coronation Hall. At the other end of the section there is also the Colour Gallery in Great Bedwyn (07760 267421).

Sports and physical recreation venues include Hungerford Leisure Centre where there is a 25m swimming pool, a fitness gym and sports hall and the private Kintbury Jubilee Sports Centre on the Inkpen Road (01488 658076) and Herongate Leisure Centre in Hungerford (01488 682000).

Nightlife is thin on this section, although the Hungerford Jazz Forum which meets at the British Legion gives players and singers of all levels an opportunity to play before a live audience in a forgiving environment. The Pelican Inn in Froxfield (01488 682479) also hosts live music on Sundays.

SECTION C

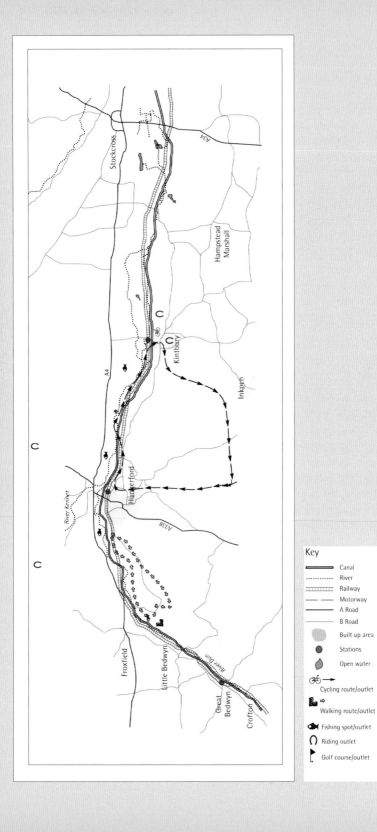

Key

Canal

River

Railway

Motorway

A Road

B Road

Built up area

Stations

Open water

Cycling route/outlet

Walking route/outlet

Fishing spot/outlet

Riding outlet

Golf course/outlet

SAMPLING

INTRODUCTION

K intbury is something of a magnet for walkers and fishermen with its clear waters and picturesque scenery. Further east at Hungerford the chalk streams of the Dun and Kennet meet, with the latter finally leaving the canal which now follows the valley of the Dun southward.

Hungerford is the natural focus of the section and offers plenty of places to park and wander, including its two expansive commons. There is a pleasant stroll to be had following the Dun down to Crofton although transport options back to your starting point are limited with the relative paucity of such options characteristic of the stretch with its large open areas of woodland and relatively few villages.

The OS Explorer Maps covering this stretch are No.158, Newbury and Hungerford and No.157, Marlborough.

WALKING

T his is an area of commons and woodlands, many of which are suitable for a short stroll. There is also a short way-marked circular walk taking in Lower Green to the west of Inkpen and the Lambourn Valley Way which cuts across the north east of Stockcross.

Both Hungerford Common to the west of the town and Hungerford Port Down to the east, south of the canal, are criss-crossed with footpaths, and these are both perfect spots to blow away the cobwebs.

Walk C takes in part of the first of these and allows you to sample the charming village of Little Bedwyn, as well as a stretch of the canal. Unusually for this section, it also has the virtue of being relatively, but not completely, flat.

SECTION C WALK
To the edge of Hungerford and Back

Description:	*A flat(ish) walk sampling the canal and Hungerford Common along roads and fields.*
Distance:	*5 miles*
Duration:	*2hrs*
Staring point:	*Grid Reference 299672, OS Explorer 158*
Nearest refreshment:	*The Harrow, Little Bedwyn*

Use the parking by Lock 68 off the minor road heading north east out of Little Bedwyn. Follow the towpath to Cobblers Lock (No.72) on the edge of the Common. Just after the lock pick up the footpath on your right over a stile and head half right over the meadow to some steps which take you up and over the railway.

> *On the other side of the railway, bear right along the edge of a field. Halfway up a small hill the path diverts to the right onto a track. At a T-junction pick up a fresh path to the left and follow this through trees until you reach a crossroads where you turn right. Stick with the road as it climbs a gentle rise, bearing left until it meets a junction and then almost immediately to the right. Pick up the footpath shortly after on the right and follow this in a straight line all the way to Little Bedwyn, bringing you out opposite the Harrow pub.*
>
> *After the pub go down the hill to rejoin the canal, picking up the towpath before the bridge and following this back to your starting point.*

There are no walking equipment outlets along this section, the nearest being in Newbury (see Section B).

CYCLING

Whilst there are a few minor roads along the south of this section, these tend to cut across the side of the Kennet Valley. The A4, meanwhile, dominates routes to the north. It is possible to construct some reasonable rides, however, and a suggested route for sampling this section by bike is to start at the parking area in Kintbury Station and head south, over the canal and past the post office. At the junction with the third road on your right, take the track heading south. This takes you to Titcomb Manor, shortly after which you pick up another minor road for 100 yards, the route becoming quite steep at this point, before picking up a fresh track and coming out on a road.

Turn right here and pick up Folly Road on your right which becomes Weavers Lane and leads you into Lower Green. Continue straight ahead for a few yards and then head right, picking up the track on the right shortly afterwards (Bitham Lane). Stay with this until you reach another track on your right, heading north.

Take this and follow it downhill until you reach a junction with another path on your left, which is actually more of a track leading to Anvilles. Stick with this all the way down to Cold Harbour where you join up with a road. Turn left here and stick with the road through Hungerford Port Down until you reach a T-junction where you turn right. Follow this to another T-junction where you head left and over the canal by a lock. Pick up the towpath and head right, staying with the canal until you reach Kintbury again – a total of around 11 miles.

There are no cycle outlets along this section, the nearest shops being in Newbury.

RIDING

The network of country roads and paths make this a popular area for riders. Many of the paths are, in fact, more like tracks and provide solid

Hungerford Wharf.

surfaces. Formal bridleways tend to be thinner on the ground however, with what there is tending to be short lengths linking other routes.

Horse-riding establishments and outlets along this section include:
- Little Hidden Farm, Hungerford (01488 683253) – *riding school*
- East Soley Equestrian Centre, Hungerford (01488 686232)
- Kintbury Park Farm, Kintbury
- L. Jenkins Livery, Kintbury (01488 658585)

FISHING

Given the confluence of the rivers Dun and Kennet as well as the presence of the canal, it is no surprise to learn that this is a favoured stretch for fishing, both for coarse anglers and game fishermen.

The most significant association with regard to the canal is the Hungerford Canal Angling Association (01672 540177), although the Reading and District AA also has a stretch at Little Bedwyn and the Civil Service AA has the rights to over half a mile of the canal along two stretches near Kintbury. There are good catches of roach, perch, grayling chub along with the occasional carp and bream.

> The waters below Hungerford Common can reward the casual visitor with sightings of wildlife varying from kingfishers and herons to water voles.

The river waters passing through Hungerford are controlled by the Commoners of that town and these are rights they guard jealously, so it is best to respect them. Elsewhere the chalk streams of the Kennet and Dun are particularly attractive to trout fishermen, especially those seeking the elusive wild Kennet trout with its distinctive butter yellow belly.

Barton Court Fisheries (01499 659094) appeals to both coarse and fly fishermen, with 3½ miles of the Kennet around Kintbury offering roach,

Kintbury Lock looking west.

dace, perch, bream pike and chub. They also have a 3-acre lake north of Kintbury well stocked with tench, bream and carp. Brown and rainbow trout can also be fished from their rivers.

The Denford Fishery at Lower Denford near Hungerford (01488 658359) is a more established trout fishery with good brown trout and regular stockings of rainbows as well as natural graylings.

Surprisingly perhaps, this stretch has no outlets selling fishing supplies.

OTHER

Of equal surprise is the fact that there is no golf course along this stretch. The closest you can get to a round is the Hungerford Leisure Centre where there is a golf simulator which allows you to play any one of thirty international courses!

CROFTON TO DEVIZES

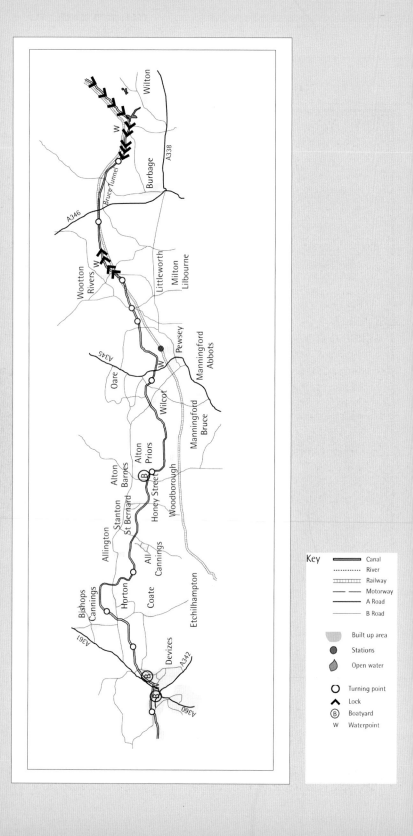

Key

	Canal
	River
	Railway
	Motorway
	A Road
	B Road

Built up area

Stations

Open water

○ Turning point

∧ Lock

Ⓑ Boatyard

W Waterpoint

SHAPERS

THE CANAL ON THIS STRETCH

KEY FACTS

LENGTH   18½ miles

BOATYARDS: 3
- Honey Street
- Devizes Marina
- Devizes Narrowboat Builders

WATERPOINTS: 4
- Crofton
- Cadley Lock
- Pewsey Wharf
- Devizes Wharf

TURNING POINTS: 11
- Wolfhall Fields Bridge
- Burbage Wharf
- Wootton Rivers Farm Bridge
- New Mill Bridge
- Milkhouse Water
- Stowell Park
- Honey Street
- Allington
- Bishop's Cannings
- Devizes Marina
- Devizes Wharf

LOCKS: 13
- Crofton Flight (9 locks – 61ft)
- Cadley Lock (8ft)
- Brimslade Lock (7ft 11in)
- Heathey Close Lock (8ft 1in)
- Wootton Rivers Bottom Lock (8ft)

The Crofton Flight is soon followed by the canal's summit and the Bruce Tunnel and a further run of four locks after which all becomes quiet as the canal begins its long lockless journey to Devizes. The Vale of Pewsey dominates the landscape, with its chalk horses and undulating ground whilst the River Avon also rises here and soon becomes a companion all the way to Bath.

After Bedwyn, it is not long before the distinctive chimney of the Crofton Pumping Station appears on the right, providing a fitting landmark for this section of the waterway. The towpath remains uneven and narrow after the locks and the run up to the Bruce Tunnel and, although mooring is possible, it is ill-advised, given the proximity of the railway.

There is a footpath over the tunnel, after which is a long, straight section down to Burbage Wharf and Wootton Top Lock, the first of four grouped into two pairs, which bring you down to Wootton Rivers. Wootton Bottom Lock is guarded by a large willow on one side and a Lock House on the other and also provides a convenient access point to this charming village.

The good news for boaters is that these locks are the last before the highly welcome '15-mile pound' of lock-free boating. This is also welcome for others enjoying the towpath as the landscape undergoes a distinct change here with the beginnings of the chalk downs of the Pewsey Vale which characterise this part of Wiltshire.

> The Bruce Tunnel was built with a wide bore to accommodate Newbury Barges and is 450ft above sea level. Thomas Bruce, after whom the tunnel is named, was the first Earl of Ailsbury.

The pound itself begins with a run of long-term moorings, with the towpath remaining turf rather than being made up. One of the by-now famous long straights precedes Carrel Crown Bridge with another following with New Mill Bridge in its centre. Here the railway moves off to the left and the canal is raised on an embankment that occasionally accentuates the view of the downs to the right.

The run into Pewsey Wharf is smooth with 48-hour moorings before a pub and a long line of craft belonging to the local boat club on the left. Pewsey can be accessed here but is a good three quarters of a mile away, although a bus connects the wharf to the town and other local points.

More boat club moorings follow the other side of the bridge after which the route becomes enclosed with trees, with the towpath crossing sides at Bristow Bridge, shortly after which there is a mile-long straight, long even by the standards of this canal. This goes past Wilcot, with the towpath becoming ever firmer and easy going with views looking out onto pastures and farmland.

Occasional glimpses of the chalk downs on the right can be gained as the canal skirts the base of the distinctive Pickled Hill, which looks almost man-made. At the beginning of this is the unusual stretch of wide water created at the insistence of Lady Susannah Wroughton when the canal was first being cut, and her memory is also preserved on Lady's Bridge that marks the end of the water. Although wide, the water is quite shallow to the left and boaters need to take care. It is worth going slowly, anyway, as there is often plenty of birdlife on display for the keen-eyed.

After some private moorings the canal sticks closely to the contour, with open fields and a steady slope up to another peak on the right, with woods down below to the left. The towpath crosses back to the left at Woodborough Fields Bridge, after which it soon becomes possible to catch a glimpse of the Alton Barnes White Horse to the right. A slight diversion here takes you to a stone memorial to a glider pilot who lost his life during the war when the plane towing him came down out of fog to find out where he was, not realising just how low he was flying.

A long line of moorings and a pub follow the friendly boatyard at the deliciously named Honey Street, a compact canalside hamlet incorporating the waterside Barge Inn. Trees and high hedges conspire to hide the view but occasional glimpses can still be had of the persistent white horse on your right. This is an extremely rural section of the canal, not only lockless, but largely bridgeless, too.

> The Barge at Honey Street is well known as a sort of museum of crop circles, this being a popular phenomenon around these parts. The walls of the pub log recent sightings and have a number of photographs.

There is a long run of decent 48-hour moorings before Bridge 127 alongside All Cannings, after which there are some splendid views of the chalk downs to the right. Allington Swing Bridge (No.118) acts as a wake-up call and provides a little light relief on the run-in to Devizes, after which the views are for once mainly to the left and take in distant hills.

A combination of reeds and rushes bring the canal down to single file in places, but adds to the variety of different greens on view. Huge fields now dominate the landscape and a long straight ends with Bishops Cannings Swing Bridge (No.133). Not long after this there is a run of formal moorings, including some next to the Bridge Inn by Bridge No.134.

More bends follow, with the canal sitting in a slight cutting, although there are views to either side, those to the right being the most distinctive. The heavily rural scene continues with another white horse briefly visible on the right near Bridge No.135.

A marina and a splash of bright red-brick housing heralds the outskirts of Devizes. The towpath becomes more solid from here and the views are mostly of the back gardens of town houses. A final swing round to the right brings you across the north of the town and alongside the old wharf, now a theatre, where there is a long run of moorings and a waterpoint just after the bridge. Boaters need to be wary of over-running for fear of entering the long flight of locks that follows soon after. Devizes itself is easily accessed either from the Wharf Bridge or the one slightly further down just after the first lock.

> Devizes Wharf hosts the headquarters of the Kennet & Avon Canal Trust, with an informative museum and the opportunity to buy a certificate for those who tame the Caen Hill flight.

PRINCIPAL TOWNS AND VILLAGES ALONG THIS STRETCH

ALLINGTON
A small hamlet dominated by a large farm.

ALL CANNINGS
A spread-out village with two greens, the northernmost of which has a Millennium Stone, whilst the latter hosts a large recreation ground. In between is a range of buildings indicating steady growth over the years.

ALTON BARNES AND PRIORS
Two adjacent hamlets notable for giving their name to the clearly visible white horse nearby. Alton Barnes' twelfth-century Saxon church is worth a visit.

BISHOPS CANNINGS
The spire of St Mary the Virgin, along with the pub, form the heart of this village off the main road.

BURBAGE
A stretched-out village of mainly modern housing, although the odd thatched cottage remains.

COATE
An impressive cricket pitch and the local pub stand out in this otherwise unremarkable village.

DEVIZES
A sleepy market town not without charms, with its wide square and main street particularly distinctive as are the site of the old Wadworth Brewery and

> Devizes is thought to take its name from the fact that ownership of the town was divided between the king and the bishops of Salisbury.

the canal itself, which weaves a path down the side of the town.

ETCHILHAMPTON
A large main house and its surroundings at one end and some rather utilitarian housing at the other make Etchilhampton something of a curate's egg.

HONEY STREET
A classic canalside village, complete with wharf and pub, which retains a dynamic 'lived in' look and feel.

HORTON
A small agricultural village with a pair of attractive half-timbered houses on its eastern side.

THE MANNINGFORDS
A collection of farming villages encompassing Maningford itself, Manningford Bruce and Manningford Abbots clustered around the upper reaches of the River Avon, which here is little more than a stream.

MILTON LILBOURNE
Tucked away off the main road, Milton Lilbourne is clustered around its Main House and the church.

OARE
A small hamlet on the A345 with its old Main House as its most distinguishing feature.

PEWSEY
A good solid market town with basic services sited a decent walk out from the canal wharf that bears its name, Pewsey evidences a strong community spirit in its annual fortnight-long carnival held in September. Its main claim to fame otherwise is that it acts as the railway halt for the surrounding area.

> The Pewsey Carnival was originally designed to raise funds for Savernake Hospital.

STANTON ST BERNARD
A small, mainly farming, community where thatched and 1960s cottages juxtapose.

WILCOT
A charming village bisected by the canal, also famous for its annual carnival.

WILTON
Not to be confused with its more famous namesake to the south, a pretty village of thatched cottages along with a pond, a pub and a windmill.

WOODBOROUGH
A dispersed village with a garden centre on its edge but little else to recommend it.

WOOTTON RIVERS
A typical linear village heading north up from a lock in the canal.

HISTORY

Although much of Wiltshire is known for its ancient antecedents, many of the settlements along this stretch have a more modest history. That said, the various hill tops peppering the Vale of Pewsey were almost destined to become Iron Age forts and the Saxons also have an illustrious connection with the surrounding area, a link commemorated in Pewsey with a statue of Alfred the Great.

This section is defined to the east by Wilton and to the west by Devizes. Roughly halfway through this section sits Pewsey, which

SECTION D

dates back to pre-Conquest times and was owned by King Alfred during the ninth century, which accounts for the statue. In 940 the estate was given to the Abbey of St Peter at Winchester and the town stayed much the same size, around 400 people, through most of the medieval age.

Pewsey's failure to develop beyond subsistence farming can probably be put down to its lack of a market, with nearby Upavon holding that privilege, although it did exploit its waterside location through development of mills. Some salvation came when the railway arrived. Although branch lines were established the prize for being the halt on the main London line fell to Pewsey, an honour it retains to this day.

Another settlement of some importance, although this may not be so apparent today, was All Cannings, west of Devizes. First settled by members of the Cana tribe in the sixth century, the area they carved out encompassed much of modern Bishop's Cannings, Allington and Etchilhampton. This grew after the Conquest to become one of the largest villages in the Vale of Pewsey and did not really decline in size until the nineteenth century when the canal came and cut it in two.

Other settlements along this stretch include Alton Barnes and Alton Priors as well as Burbage, and although the origins of these can be traced back to Saxon times, their histories have, by and large, been unspectacular.

Devizes began to gain prominence around the time of the Domesday Book, its status helped by the erection of a Norman castle built by Osmund, Bishop of Salisbury. Originally built of wood, this burned down in 1113, being rebuilt in stone by Roger of Salisbury, Osmund's successor.

The castle became the focal point of Devizes' history for the next century, changing hands many times during the civil war between Stephen and Matilda, with the latter's gratitude leading to the granting of a charter to hold regular markets thereby securing subsequent prosperity. Streets emerged to house craftsmen and traders outside the castle walls and Devizes achieved sufficient status to send two representatives to Edward I's model Parliament in 1295.

The next Civil War was to prove less rewarding. The town's position between the king's stronghold in Oxford and supporters in the south-west made Devizes a strategic spot. In 1642 the town was besieged by the Parliamentary forces, eventually being relieved by forces sent from Oxford and a rout followed at nearby Roundway Hill, with Devizes remaining Royalist for a further two years.

Devizes' position as a market centre, once the largest in the west of England for corn, was celebrated in 1815, nearly 600 years after the first recorded market in the town, with the erection of a large market cross which cost a princely £2,000, a sum put up by Lord Sidmouth.

It fell to Oliver Cromwell himself to take Devizes, something he did with relative ease when a single cannon shot landed near the keep where the Royalists' gunpowder was kept. Although it failed to explode, the Royalists wisely chose to surrender.

After the war the castle was destroyed and Devizes returned to its market, which in the sixteenth and seventeenth centuries majored in cheese, bacon and butter, as well as fish brought up from Poole. Later on, Devizes became a centre for wool, with silk and the weaving of crape, a silk used for mourning clothes. Brewing and snuff manufacture also helped boost the town's economy which was further helped by the coming of the canal which linked Devizes to Bristol and London, two of the country's four main seaports.

The town's wharf became a distribution centre for coal from Somerset, as well as a place from which to send its beer to London. Tobacco for the snuff business also came from Bristol via the West Indies. Devizes was less lucky with railways, however. Caen Hill outside the town had been tamed by the canal but proved too much for Brunel and his men, with the great engineer preferring the simpler route between Swindon and Chippenham.

THE NATURAL LANDSCAPE

The landscape along this stretch is dominated by the North Wessex Downs and the Marlborough Downs to the north and the northern limit of Salisbury Plain to the south. The Vale of Pewsey across the middle runs roughly east to west, eventually merging with the Kennet Valley.

The canal is able to stay flat by following an at times snaking route as it seeks to avoid both small villages and distinctive hills, such as Clifford's Hill to the east of Allington, which rises to nearly 800ft. Other than the canal, water is scarce, due largely to the chalk slopes.

SECTION D

Lady's Bridge.

Make the most of the Savernake Forest and Bedwyn Common to the north if you like woodland, as once you get past Burbage Wharf the landscape becomes one of rolling hills, although the odd copse peppers the sides.

ACCESS AND TRANSPORT

ROADS

Three A roads divide this section vertically, the A346 which passes through Burbage, the A345 which takes in Pewsey and the A361 which passes through the top of Devizes. Along with these there is also the A338 which cuts an east/west path across the bottom of the section and links up with the B3087 Burbage Road to provide a link between Burbage and Pewsey.

Devizes also acts as something of a junction point for A roads with the A360 and A342 passing through it. Otherwise, the area to the south of the canal tends to be better connected.

> 2006 marks the centenary of direct rail links between Pewsey and London.

RAIL

Since 1966, when the station at Devizes was closed, Pewsey has had the distinction of having the only station in this section, from where there is a regular service linking London to Bristol, with the former only around an hour distant.

Services are run by First Great Western (0845 6005604) but for more detailed information contact National Train Enquiries on 08457 484950 or www.nationalrail.co.uk.

BUSES

The following list sets out the main bus services on this section although it is advisable to check before using them as some buses only run on certain days and others may have been withdrawn since publication of this Guide. It is also worth checking for more local services, especially within Devizes.

- 5/6 – *Salisbury to Marlborough/Swindon via Pewsey (W&D)*
- 12 – *Pewsey to Devizes via Woodborough (W&D)*
- 13 – *Pewsey to Wilcot. Tuesday only (Pewsey Coaches)*
- 17 – *Marlborough circular, takes in Burbage and Wootton Rivers (W&D)*
- 18 – *Pewsey circular service to surrounding villages (W&D)*
- 19 – *Pewsey to Marlborough via Wootton Rivers (W&D)*
- 20 – *Bedwyn to Pewsey via Oare (W&D)*
- 21 – *Pewsey to Marlborough via Burbage and Wilton (W&D)*
- 22/22A/23 – *Hungerford to Marlborough via Wilton and Burbage (W&D)*
- 49 – *Devizes to Swindon via Bishops Cannings (Thamesdown Transport)*

- 80 – *Etchilhampton to Devizes via Bishops Cannings and Coate (Bodmans Coaches)*
- 211 – *Enford to Pewsey via Manningford Bruce, Woodborough, Alton Barnes, Alton Priors and Wilcot. School terms only (Tourist Coaches)*
- 249 – *Pewsey to Devizes via Woodborough (Tourist Coaches)*
- WB4 – *Devizes to Great Bedwyn via Pewsey. Saturday only (Hatts Coaches)*
- WB8 – *Pewsey local service (Hatts Coaches)*
- WB10 – *Pewsey to Devizes (Hatts Coaches)*
- WB11 – *Pewsey to Devizes via Wilcot, Alton Barnes, All Cannings, Allington, Horton and Coate (Hatts Coaches)*

In addition, the National Express coach service 402 links Trowbridge, Melksham, Devizes, Hungerford and Newbury on its way into London once every day of the week, passing through a number of the sections covered in this Guide.

Contact details for bus operators in this area are listed below, although Traveline (www.traveline.org.uk) on 0870 6082608 can give details of specific services between 7 a.m. and 10 p.m.:

- Bodmans Coaches, Worton (01380 722393)
- Hatts Coaches, Chippenham (01249 740444)
- Pewsey Coaches, Pewsey (01672 562238)
- Thamesdown Transport, Swindon (01793 428428)
- Tourist Coaches, Salisbury (01722 338359)
- W&D – Wilts and Dorset Bus Co., Poole (01202 678291)

TAXIS

The following list gives a selection of the taxi operators in this section:

- A2B Taxis, Pewsey (01672 562291)
- Ace Taxis, Devizes (01380 729629)
- Devizes Taxis, Devizes (01380 723129)
- Roy's Taxis, Burbage (01672 811533)
- Taylor Taxis, Pewsey (01672 562197)
- RH Reeves, Rowde (01380 725072)

SECTION D

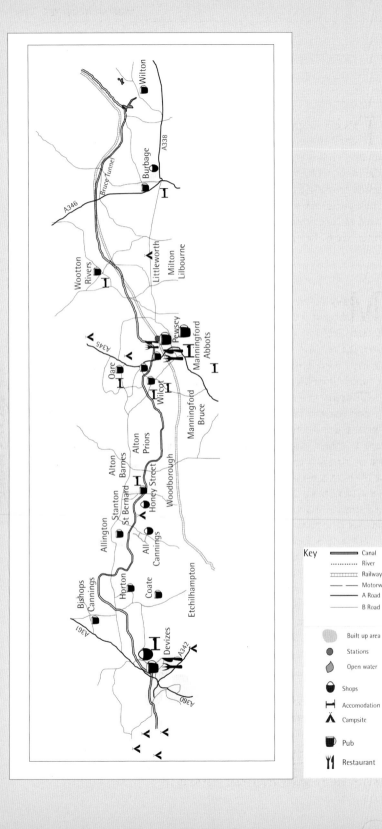

Key

Canal	
River	
Railway	
Motorway	
A Road	
B Road	

Built up area

Stations

Open water

Shops

Accomodation

Campsite

Pub

Restaurant

BASICS

INTRODUCTION

This is a sleepy section of the towpath, characterised by a number of small scattered communities with the small town of Pewsey in the middle, ending up at Devizes. Most of these communities are near or on the canal, with the Vale of Pewsey to the north and Salisbury Plain to the south providing effective geographical barriers to development. Whilst there are a number of pubs dotted along the towpath, like the shops you need to take advantage of them when you can although Devizes fulfils most needs. Devizes also has a community hospital (01380 723511).

SHOPPING

Many of the villages scattered about this section are too small to support a shop of their own, although there are exceptions. These include Burbage, which has both a post office and a separate village stores, and All Cannings, which has a post office. Otherwise, the retail opportunities in these communities vary from oriental antiques (Manningford) through a Country Store (Honey Street) and a garden centre (Woodborough).

Shopping in Pewsey is probably best described as eclectic, although it does have a large Co-op in its centre. Basic services include Lloyds Bank, a newsagent and a pharmacy, along with a post office in the centre and a Londis. Notable exceptions include an excellent bakery, a rather up-market deli hidden around the corner and an art shop. There is also a WI market every Tuesday morning in the Bouverie Hall. Devizes wears its market town status on its sleeve, with a large open area which hosts a Farmers' Market on the first Saturday of every month, a large indoor market (Thursday to Saturday) and an antiques market on Tuesdays.

There is a Tesco in the town centre and a Somerfield on the outskirts as well as a Safeway and a Budgens. There is also a full range of banks, pharmacists, butchers, bakers, bookshops and hardware shops. The shops are scattered in Devizes and it can be easy to lose your bearings, although most routes bring you back to either the market square or main car park. Heading out of town there is a useful Spar off the left just as the locks begin to get into their stride.

EATING AND DRINKING

There is a reasonable selection of pubs along this section, many of which are canalside, with those at Honey Street and All Cannings all particularly convenient. Other than Devizes, Pewsey offers the greatest concentration of pubs, although these are a good walk away from the canal.

Being a market town, Devizes has a number of watering holes of which the following represents a selection:

SECTION D

- Artichoke (01380 723400) –
- Black Horse (01380 723930)
- Bridge Inn (01380 860273)
- British Lion (01380 720665)
- Crown (01380 722692)
- George and Dragon (01380 723053)
- New Inn (01380 860644)
- Pelican (01380 723909)
- Royal Oak (01380 728608)

Otherwise, the following pubs are all accessible from the towpath:

- The Swan Inn, Wilton (01672 870274)
- Three Horseshoes, Burbage (01672 810324)
- White Hart, Burbage (01672 810336)
- Royal Oak, Wootton Rivers (01672 810322)
- Coopers Arms, Pewsey (01672 562495)
- The Crown, Pewsey (01380 860218)
- French Horn, Pewsey (01672 562443) – *wharfside*
- Greyhound, Pewsey (01672 564445)
- Moonrakers, Pewsey (01672 562585)
- Royal Oak, Pewsey (01672 563426)
- Waterfront, Pewsey (01672 564020) – *wharfside*
- White Hart, Oare (01672 562273)
- Golden Swan, Wilcot (01672 562289)
- Barge Inn, Honey Street (01672 851705)
- Kings Arms, All Cannings (01380 860328)
- Crown, Bishops Cannings (01380 860218)
- Bridge Inn, Horton (01380 860273)
- New Inn, Coate (01380 860644)

Devizes is not overly blessed with places to eat, but after the paucity of opportunity in the preceding miles it still represents something of an oasis. Options include:

- Bejing Paradise (01380 723009) – *Chinese*
- Franco's (01380 724007) – *Italian*
- Deedar (01380 720009) – *Indian*
- Tino's Pizzeria (01380 722446) – *Italian*
- Wharfside Restaurant (01380 726051)

Outside of Devizes, when it comes to eating it is best to aim for the pubs, although Pewsey has a small selection of restaurants:

- Chequers Bistro, Pewsey (01672 564004)
- The Dragon Inn, Pewsey (01672 563777) – *Thai, fish and chips*
- Shanty Tandoori, Pewsey (01672 564640)
- Pewsey Takeaway (01672 569069)

Devizes is also good for teas, with the Quintessence Tea Rooms (01380 722693) and the Caen Hill Café and Information Centre, Devizes (01380 318000), halfway down the flight, accessible by road from the bottom. The

Waterfront on Pewsey Wharf (01672 564020) does cream teas and snacks as does Pewsey Vale Crafts and Tea Room (01672 563823) in the town.

SLEEPING

The only hotels in this section are in Devizes, with a choice of three:

- The Bear Hotel, Devizes (01380 722450) – *recently refurbished historic hotel*
- The Black Swan, Devizes (01380 723259) – *seventeenth-century coaching inn*
- The Castle Hotel, Devizes (01380 729300) – *eighteenth-century coaching inn*

Outside of Devizes bed and breakfasts are the best bet for somewhere to stay along this section, with the following list offering a selection of possible options, many of which are in farmhouse settings or in pubs:

- The Artichoke, Devizes (01380 723400)
- Bramley House, Devizes (01380 729444)
- Greenfields, Devizes (01380 729315)
- Roundway Farm House, Devizes (01380 723113)
- Upper Westcourt, Burbage (01672 810307)
- Royal Oak, Wootton Rivers (01672 810322)
- The Royal Oak, Pewsey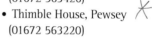
- (01672 563426)
- Thimble House, Pewsey (01672 563220)
- Huntlys Farm, Manningford Abbots (01672 563663)
- The Golden Swan, Wilcot (01672 562289)
- Wilcot Lodge, Wilcot (01672 563465)
- Well Cottage, Honey Street (01672 851577)
- White Hart, Oare (01672 562248)

CAMPING

A number of places offer pitches for camping on this section, including:

- Wernham Farm (01672 512236) – *camping and B&B a little north of Pewsey Wharf*
- Hillview Park, Oare (01672 563151) – *family-run site off*
- A345 with ten pitches
- The Barge Inn, Honey Street (01672 851705)
- Bell Caravan Park, Devizes (01380 722767)

Camping is also possible in the Savernake Forest. Bucklands in Devizes (01380 722784) is the sole camping supplies outlet.

SECTION D

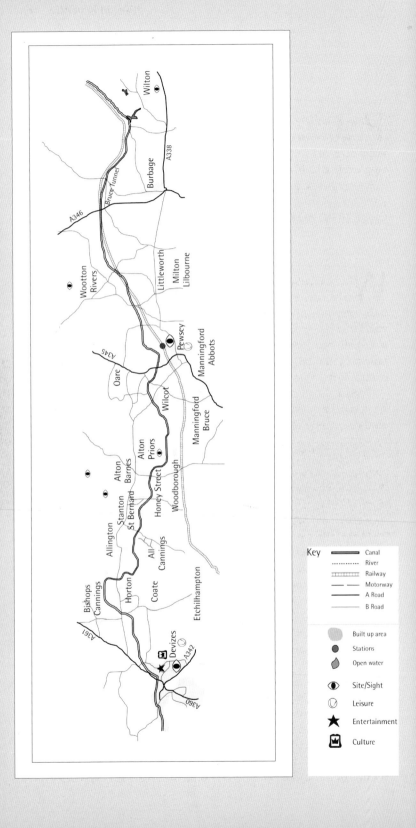

Key

	Canal
	River
	Railway
	Motorway
	A Road
	B Road

Built up area
Stations
Open water

Site/Sight
Leisure
Entertainment
Culture

SEEING AND DOING

INTRODUCTION

Pewsey and Devizes are the main foci along this stretch, although the Vale of Pewsey itself, with its various small villages, is an attraction in its own right with nature reserves, white horses and the occasional crop circle all adding to the interest.

Pewsey has a small information point with basic tourist information (01672 564364), whilst Devizes has a more fully fledged Tourist Information Centre (01380 729408) conveniently located in the Market Square.

SIGHTS

Wilton Windmill (01672 870266) is open from 2 to 5 on Sundays and Bank Holidays and owes its existence to the canal as it was built when the River Bedwyn, which previously powered a number of water mills, was canalised during the cutting of the canal. The mill is a traditional tower mill with a fantail which turns the Cap and has four sails in total, two patent, which can be quickly activated and two common canvas sails, which have to be set before the mill starts to turn.

If passing through Wootton Rivers, look out for the church clock which is unusual for having the inscription 'Glory Be To God' in place of numbers on the southerly of its three faces. The clock is run by two hand-wound lead weights, one for the clock and one for the chimes.

> The Wootton Rivers church clock was originally built using cast-off parts from agricultural machinery and, despite keeping good time for years, is slowly being replaced by fresh parts a piece at a time.

Moving on to Pewsey, it is worth a wander to spot some historical buildings in the village, notably the timber-framed cruck house at Ball Corner, Bridge Cottage on the banks of the Avon and the Court House by the church. The centre of the village has as its focus a fine statue of King Alfred whilst the church has an altar rail made from the timbers of a boat captured by Lord Nelson.

The most significant attraction in Pewsey, however, has to be the Pewsey Heritage Centre (01672 562617) housed in an old Victorian stone foundry near the bridge. The Centre is free (although donations are welcome!) and houses a collection that looks back on the social, agricultural and industrial history of the Vale of Pewsey over the last 150 years, with a particular focus on the Kennet & Avon Canal, the railway and the impact that industrialisation had on the local landscape. On the canal itself, a walk up from the village, there is a good example of one of the wharves that used to typify the canal, and perhaps just as importantly, a teashop. Canal cruises are also available from here.

To the west it is impossible to miss the Alton Barnes White Horse which dominates the skyline for a number of miles along the towpath. Sited on

SECTION D

Milk Hill about a mile south of the village after which it is named, the White Horse is one of several in the area, dating back to 1812. Another is the Pewsey White Horse, perhaps best viewed from Milk Hill, a more recent addition to the collection. In nearby Alton Priors there is a local Sarsen Stone with a carving of the Alton Barnes horse on it.

> The Pewsey Downs National Nature Reserve sits on the side of a steep south-facing slope overlooking the Vale of Pewsey and takes in the three Milk, Walkers and Knapp Hills.

Also in the vicinity is Adams Grave, a Neolithic chambered long barrow comprising a long mound with visible stones in a hollow towards the south-east, thought to be the remains of a burial chamber. Another local Neolithic site is Knapp Hill, also near to Alton Barnes, a causewayed camp with seven ditch sections where pottery has been found which dates the enclosure back to 3500BC.

Before leaving this area, the Saxon church of All Saints at Alton Priors is worth a visit, if for nothing else than to see its tall tower which stands like a beacon amongst the surrounding fields. The interior is almost barn-like with its lime-washed walls and large roof trusses. Look out for the Jacobean pews, unusually tall communion rails and a tomb that dates back to 1590. The Barge Inn at Honey Street (01672 851705) has already been mentioned and has an international reputation for its displays of photographs and reports of local crop circles (see 'Learn More and Links').

Devizes acts as a natural terminus for this section and offers a good selection of attractions. There are two museums here of note, with the Kennet & Avon Canal Museum (01380 729489) probably of most interest to towpath travellers. This is located, appropriately enough, on the wharf and tells the story of the canal from 1794 to the present day. There is also a gift shop and a tea shop. It is also possible to hire day boats from the nearby Devizes Marina (01380 725300), from the wharf (White Horse Boats 01380 728504) and from the Barge at Honey Street.

The second museum is the Wiltshire Heritage Museum (01380 727369), which has what

> Those who have successfully negotiated the Caen Hill flight can buy a certificate marking their achievement from the Canal Museum.

many regard to be one of the best collections of Bronze Age artefacts outside London. Founded in 1853 following the acquisition of the John Britton library of topographical and antiquarian books and manuscripts by a group of Wiltshire gentlemen (mainly clergymen and local gentry), the inaugural meeting resolved, 'to cultivate and collect information on archaeology and Natural History in their various branches and to form a Library and Museum illustrating the history, natural, civic and ecclesiastic of the County of Wilts'.

There are also plenty of buildings in Devizes worth taking in, including The Bear Hotel, the Corn Exchange and Town Hall overlooking the Market Square, timbered buildings in St Johns Alley that date back to the 1500s and a number of fine Georgian edifices. It is also impossible to miss (or even smell the outputs from) the magnificent Victorian façade of the Wadworth Brewery near the centre of the town. The Caen Hill flight is also, of course, a significant visitor draw.

> The Market Cross in Devizes bears an inscription about Ruth Pierce, a local woman who died suddenly after cheating in the market – a warning to anyone who may be tempted to follow in her footsteps.

Devizes is not without its own historical remnants, including what remains of its castle and, dating much further back, the Marden Henge, which is the oldest henge in Britain, enclosing 14 hectares – two and a half more than nearby Avebury, although it is much less impressive to look at. Also known as the Hatfield Earthworks, the henge comprises a bank and internal ditch surviving on the northern and eastern sides.

> The Wadworth Brewery was founded in 1875 and if you're lucky may even see the company's Shire Horses delivering beer to local hostelries.

If the henge fails to satisfy your need for colour you can try the Broadleas Gardens (01380 722035) about a mile south of the town. This is a well-maintained 10-acre garden with interest throughout the year, although it is open only on Sundays, Wednesdays and Thursdays.

CULTURE AND ENTERTAINMENT

Devizes acts as the main focus for arts and entertainment along this section. The town is lucky to have the excellent Wharf Theatre near the Canal Museum (01380 725944) which puts on a number of shows a year ranging from a pantomime through musicals to contemporary drama. The theatre has its own company but also welcomes other local and national players, both amateur and professional.

Devizes also has a small cinema, the Regal (01380 722971) which shows mostly mainstream films. If it is arts you are after, the Wine Street Gallery in the town (01380 728387) can be worth a visit.

There are two main centres offering leisure and sporting facilities along this stretch. The first is the Pewsey Leisure Centre (01225 713000) which has a 25m pool, a sports hall, racket sport courts (including squash) and a skate park. The second is the Devizes Leisure Centre (01380 728894) which at the time of writing was in the process of being redeveloped, although it does include a swimming pool.

If you are feeling adventurous mountain boarding might fit the bill (01672 851648). As the name suggests this involves hurtling down the sides of the nearby hills on a skateboard with enlarged wheels. There are two tracks, one for beginners and another for the more advanced practitioner.

The best place for live music along this section is almost certainly the Corn Exchange in Devizes (01380 722160). There is also the Old Crown (01380 722692) which appeals more to the over-21s.

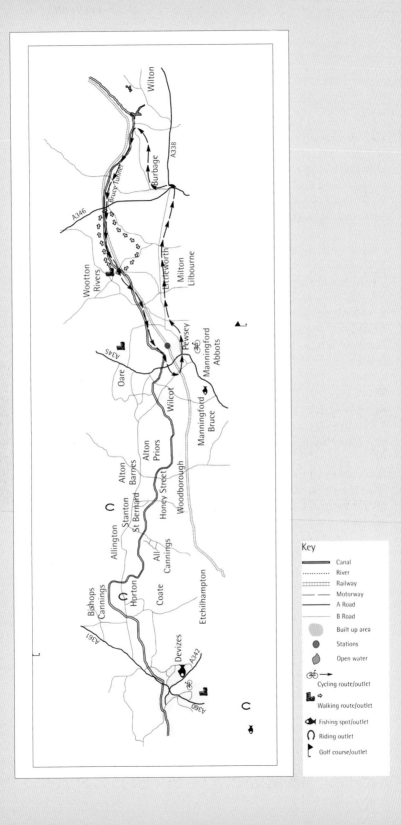

Key

— Canal
········· River
▥▥▥ Railway
— — Motorway
—— A Road
—— B Road
🟦 Built up area
🔴 Stations
🟠 Open water
🚲→ Cycling route/outlet
🏭⇨ Walking route/outlet
🐟 Fishing spot/outlet
∩ Riding outlet
⚑ Golf course/outlet

SAMPLING

INTRODUCTION

The Vale of Pewsey with its undulating views dominates this stretch, with plenty of opportunities available to dip in and enjoy the scenery. This stretch also includes the 15-mile lockless pound and is characterised by a series of pretty, small canalside villages and pubs.

The relevant OS Explorer Map is No.157, Marlborough and Savernake Forest, with some of the southern parts drifting into Explorer 130, Salisbury and Stonehenge.

WALKING

This is an area rich in walking opportunities, both formal and informal, with most of the villages offering good jumping-off points for a walk. There is a useful car park at Pewsey Wharf, although you are limited to 4 hours, and there are a couple of car parks in the Savernake Forest. For those who prefer easier paths, three town trails covering Pewsey are available from the Information Point.

Once an ancient hunting forest, the Savernake Forest north of Burbage Wharf covers 2,000 acres of woodland criss-crossed with paths and is home to wildlife such as woodpeckers, owls, badgers, foxes and deer.

Tan Hill Way, which links Gopher Wood, 2 miles due north of Wilcot, with Tan Hill, a similar distance north of Stanton St Bernard, passes over the top of the Downs, affording some spectacular views. Along the way it links up with another of the established paths in this section, the White Horse Trail, which passes by the Alton Barnes white horse and goes through the heart of Pewsey. Just to the north of both of these sits the Wansdyke Path.

Jones Mill Nature Reserve just to the north of Pewsey is Wiltshire's only fenland reserve. Belted Galloway cattle graze the wet meadows where there are plenty of well-marked (if occasionally rather damp!) paths. Finally, there are a number of paths to the east of Devizes, including the Wessex Ridgeway which skirts Etchilhampton Hill.

Walk D has been designed to allow the walker to sample the last of locks before the beginning of the 15-mile pound.

SECTION D

SECTION D WALK
Wootton Rivers and Burbage Wharf

Description:	*A slight climb amongst fields.*
Distance:	*3½ miles*
Duration:	*1¼hrs*
Staring point:	*Grid Reference 197633, OS Explorer 157*
Nearest refreshment:	*Royal Oak, Wootton Rivers*

Park by the pub and head down to the canal, heading left at the lock on the far side of the bridge. Follow the towpath eastwards past three more locks until you reach a footpath heading right just before the start of some trees. Head up this and immediately left, into and out of the copse, following the path as it bends sharply right and up a track to a road into Ram Alley.

Turn right at the road and walk up Dark Dale until you reach a crossroad of paths after about a third of a mile at the top of the hill. Pick up the right-hand option, which soon heads downhill, bending to the right as it does so, following the right-hand edge of a field. The path diverts to the left after a small clump of trees and soon joins up with a minor road, where you turn right. Follow this down the hill and you will arrive back at the Wootton Rivers Bridge, where you head back to your starting point.

Walking equipment outlets along this section include:
• Bucklands, Devizes (01380 722784)

CYCLING

The profusion of minor roads makes for easy cycling along this stretch, although the towpath is not always forgiving. In addition, National Cycle Route 4 weaves its way along the northern part of the Vale of Pewsey.

To sample part of this section on two wheels, first head east out of Pewsey on the Burbage Road (B3087) past Littleworth and the camping at Greenacres all the way to Burbage itself. Turn left at the roundabout and down the High Street, until you reach a crossroads with Wolfhall Road on the right. Take this to Wolfhall Manor and Farm, where the road briefly becomes a track and bears right.

Stick with it (you are now on Cycle Route 4), until you reach the canal at Freewarren Bridge, opposite Crofton Pumping Station. Pick up the towpath here, heading left. Pass up and over the Bruce Tunnel and past Burbage Wharf all the way to Pewsey Wharf, a distance of around 7 miles. Head left on the A345 back into Pewsey – a total distance of around 17 miles.

Cycle outlets along this section include:
• Bikes and Boards, Devizes (01380 729621)

RIDING

As well as the formal paths listed above, there are a number of bridleways along this section, with one heading south-east out of All Cannings and another north-west out of the same village via Allington. The path along Mud Lane, which links up with Tan Hill Way and starts south of the Savernake Forest, is another good route.

Horse-riding establishments and outlets along this section include:

- Horton Mill Farm Livery, Horton (01380 860458)
- Little Leaze Livery Yard, Devizes (01373 824376)
- Milton Stud, Milton Lilbourne, Pewsey (01672 562924) – *stud with show jumping and cross-country clinics*
- Pewsey Vale Riding Centre, Stanton St Bernard (01672 851400) – *stabling for over ninety horses*

FISHING

The Devizes Angling Association (01380 725189) controls fishing from the towpath along this stretch, from Lady's Bridge near Wilcot, through Pewsey and the villages east of Devizes. There is a good selection of common, mirror and crucian carp as well as roach, perch and tench along this stretch. Otherwise, contact the Pewsey & District Angling Club (01672 562541) which controls the section between Lady's Bridge near Wilcot to Milkhouse Water Bridge.

Trout fishing is also available at the Mill Farm Trout Lakes (01380 813138) where there are two 3-acre lakes, and Manningford Trout Fishery (01980 630 033) where there is a 4-acre lake and 2 miles of river fishing.

Outlets selling fishing supplies along this stretch include:
- Bernie's Bait and Tackle, Devizes (01380 730712)
- Devizes Angling, Devizes (01380 722350)

SECTION D

Part of the 15-Mile Pound.

Alton Barnes white horse.

OTHER

Not surprisingly, the Vale of Pewsey has proved attractive to golfers and there are two courses on this stretch of similar length, both offering spectacular views.

- North Wilts Golf Club, Devizes (01380 860466) – *elevated course of 6,414 yards.*

- Upavon Golf Course, Nr Pewsey (01980 630787) – *6,410 yards.*

DEVIZES TO AVONCLIFF

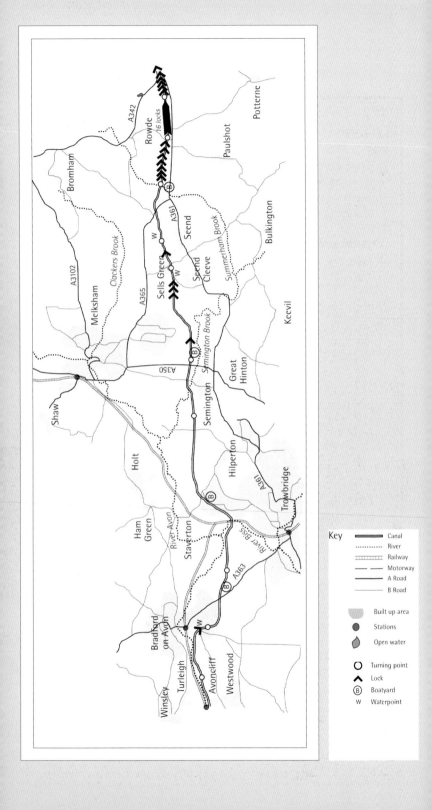

Key

━━━	Canal
········	River
▥▥▥▥	Railway
─ ─ ─	Motorway
━━━	A Road
──	B Road

🟤 Built up area

🔴 Stations

🔵 Open water

○ Turning point

∧ Lock

Ⓑ Boatyard

W Waterpoint

SHAPERS

THE CANAL ON THIS STRETCH

KEY FACTS

LENGTH: 13 miles

BOATYARDS: 4

Foxhanger Wharf, Devizes
Tranquil Boats, Semington
Wessex Narrowboats, Hilperton
Bradford on Avon Marina

WATERPOINTS: 3

Sells Green   Bradford Wharf
Barge Inn, Seend

TURNING POINTS: 10

Top of Caen Hill   Between Semington and
Bottom of Caen Hill   Whaddon
Foxhangers   Bradford Approach
Sells Green   Bradford Wharf
Seend Wharf   Barton Farm Country
Semington Wharf   Park

LOCKS: 37

Kennet Lock (8ft 2in)   Locks 22-28 (7 locks,
Maton Lock (8ft 2in)   57ft 2in)
Trust Lock (8ft 2in)   Seend Locks (5 locks,
Prison Lock (8ft 2in)   38ft 4in)
H.P. Herbert Lock   Semington Top Lock
  (8ft 2in)   (7ft 10in)
The Cave Lock (8ft 2in)   Buckley's Lock (8ft 3in)
Caen Hill (16 locks   Bradford Lock (10ft 3in)
  130ft 8in)

One of the undoubted highlights of the Kennet & Avon, the Caen Hill flight of locks, which begins this section, presents a dramatic vista whichever way you approach it. The flight takes a long time to totally unwind, but there is a quiet stretch soon after which brings towpath travellers over the top of Trowbridge and into the base of Bradford on Avon, one of the prettiest towns on the canal and a good sampler for the delights of Bath in the next section.

On the other side of Devizes begins the long descent of the Caen Hill Flight Locks, twenty-nine in total, including sixteen down the notorious hill itself, a long and steady journey offering spectacular views. Six locks of exactly the same depth break you in gently, but after that it is a steep fall. The towpath to the left is usually full of gongoozlers and just before the hill an arch in the road bridge gives them access.

The flight itself has deep side pounds to the right. These were used for sponsored races during the period when the Trust was still raising money for restoration and one of the locks is duly named in their honour. In fact, many of the locks have been named, including one after the Queen who officially reopened the canal here by travelling down the lock in question.

Boat passages down the flight can vary from 3 to 6 hours depending upon your luck, but rushing defeats the object as the flight is an experience and one to be savoured rather than simply endured. The fall is dramatic and is a challenge not only for boaters but walkers and cyclists also.

The best view of the flight is probably from the bottom just before the canal passes through the Marsh Lane Bridge, after which there are six further locks and another bridge and a boatyard with the remains of the pier of an old bridge in the middle of the water providing a distinct hazard to shipping. A wooded cutting follows, with moorings at Sells Green a good place for weary crews to stop. Water is available for those travelling by boats on the towpath and for those travelling through at the nearby Three Magpies pub past the camp site. The footpath remains solid along this stretch with flat pastures below on the right and gently rolling hills to the left. Two swing bridges punctuate the straight stretch before the intriguingly named Seend Silver Bridge, which itself sits at the beginning of a run of five locks.

The inviting Barge Inn sits in the middle of the flight, where there is also a watering point and a DIY pump-out. A run of 72-hour moorings follows at the bottom, which offers respite before a sequence of three swing bridges. Views here are mainly away to the left, where the route of Semington Brook can just be made out.

The two Semington locks end with a winding hole. This spot is notable for being the site of the junction with the old Wilts & Berks Canal, which used to run to

> The Wilts & Berks Canal was built to allow a means of ferrying coal to Oxford and London from the Somerset coalfields. It was never a commercial success as the Kennet and Avon was quicker.

Abingdon where it linked up with the Thames. A short run of 24-hour moorings follow, along with a much longer run of long-term permit holders.

Semington Aqueduct follows, with a swing bridge also named after this small village shortly afterwards, which lies slightly to the south. The canal now re-finds its previous form with a long straight, spanned by two bridges (Nos 162 and 163). Gaps through hedges allow occasional views to the right, but the canal swerves to the left and another long straight starts the long run in to the north of Trowbridge.

Mooring is possible here and it is a good quiet place to stop if you want to avoid Trowbridge, which actually lies some way to the south, the housing you can see being more accurately described as Hilperton.

Hilperton Road Bridge (No.166) marks the start of a short brush with an urban landscape, although before that the canal passes the large Hilperton Marina, home to a large hire fleet. On the towpath side the canal passes a modern development of flats, with more development promised.

Most of the evidence of a town here at all is hidden by high hedging to the left and Trowbridge vanishes from sight almost as quickly as it appeared, with the consecutive Ladydown and Bliss Aqueducts carrying the canal over the railway and the River Bliss respectively. The more significant River Avon soon begins to define the landscape to the right, creating a wide valley and flowing close to the canal after Ladydown Bridge (No.169). Only those on foot will really be able to appreciate it, however.

This is a popular recreational stretch of canal, conveniently linking the two towns of Trowbridge and Bradford on Avon. Tall trees hide the non-towpath side whilst smaller bushes and trees do an equally effective job of cutting out the view to the right.

There is a long run of 48-hour moorings on the approach to Bradford Marina, offering basic services and acting as another host for a hire fleet. Housing starts again at Bridge No.170, but only on the right, and is mainly hidden behind trees as the canal passes along a cutting. A straight stretch precedes a sharp swing to the right at Underwoods Bridge (No.171) leading in turn, quite suddenly, to Bradford Upper Wharf.

> The wide-beamed *Barbara Mclellan* operates out of Bradford Wharf and is operated by volunteers from the Kennet & Avon Trust, offering short trips, including access for the disabled (01225 782090).

> The decline in trade at Bradford Wharf was dramatic. In 1860 100,000 tons passed through; thirty years later this was only 14,000 tons.

There is mooring either side of the lock, with facilities and a water point, as well as a small shop before it. This is a very popular stopping point, being close to two pubs and some fast-food takeaways, although the town itself is only a short distance away to the right. A long run of moorings follows under trees after the lock, many of which are occupied by long-term permit holders. Those who are able can peek through the trees down onto the Avon Valley, which will now dominate the landscape between here and Bath.

The moorings continue the other side of the (normally open) Bradford Swing Bridge, where they enjoy stone sidings. The railway rediscovers its voice here, the river being not the only feature to occupy the valley. The canal, however, sits imperiously above all this, accompanied by a solid towpath, and soon the impressive Avoncliff Aqueduct carries over both the river and the railway.

PRINCIPAL TOWNS AND VILLAGES ALONG THIS STRETCH

AVONCLIFF
A small hamlet with the aqueduct that bears its name as its star.

SECTION E

BRADFORD ON AVON
Enjoying a reputation as a smaller version of Bath, Bradford on Avon is a characterful town full of alleyways and side streets with the Avon carving a majestic path through its heart, somewhat overshadowing the canal to the south.

BROMHAM
A spread-out village, Bromham has seen various stages of growth, including a recent one. The church spire acts as a beacon from some distance.

BULKINGTON
A village that has seen much modern development based around a traditional rural core.

GREAT HINTON
A small village with a pub and old red phone box at its centre.

HAM GREEN
Essentially an extension of Holt.

HILPERTON
Home to the large Alvechurch Marina, and also known as Staverton Waterside rather than the less alluring Hilperton Marsh.

HOLT
A large village with a triangular green providing the focal point.

KEEVIL
An attractive compact village of contrasting architectural styles.

MELKSHAM
Another Wiltshire market town with a proud history but a less obvious future, Melksham lacks some of the distinguishing features of its neighbours.

> Melksham has long been associated with dairy farming and its name derives from *meoloc*, the Saxon word for milk.

PAULSHOT
A small but strung out village with a pub and a large green in the centre.

POTTERNE
Balanced precariously on a steep hill with a high retaining wall down one side, Potterne's most distinguishing feature is its row of half-timbered houses at its centre.

ROWDE
Two pubs and a dairy farm are the main features of interest in this small, typical Wiltshire village.

SEEND

Neatly cut in two by the A365 with the older part lying to the south, including Seend Park.

SEEND CLEEVE

A small village with its roots still deeply in farming.

SELLS GREEN

Notable chiefly for being the location of a large canalside camping site.

SEMINGTON

A sleepy village down a no-through road leading to the canal with some elegant Georgian houses scattered amongst its cottages.

SHAW

Remarkable mainly for its church at one end and a country house hotel at the other.

STAVERTON

Dominated by a large Nestlé factory, Staverton is a small and compact village with a pub.

THURLEIGH

A small village tucked away on the hillside outside Winsley.

TROWBRIDGE

Trowbridge's most famous son is probably Sir Isaac Pitman who invented the form of shorthand that bears his name.

A large market town and regional centre boasting a long history, Trowbridge has a wide variety of shops scattered about its centre but no obvious anchor store or any of the large international chains, although further development was taking place at the time of writing.

WESTWOOD

A village combining old and new, sandwiched between Westwood Manor to the east and Ilford Manor to the west.

SECTION E

HISTORY

After Devizes it is the three textile towns of Melksham, Trowbridge and Bradford on Avon that dominate the eastern half of this section, and although all sit near enough to the canal to enjoy its benefits, only the latter has it flowing anywhere near its centre.

Melksham was originally settled to the east of the Avon and by the time of the Domesday Book was a large estate held by the crown, with the Avon first bridged in the early fifteenth century. Like many other local towns, Melksham owes much to the granting of a right to hold a market, in this case a privilege first granted in 1219.

Perhaps more oddly, at one time Melksham aspired to be a spa town along the lines of nearby Bath. Two mineral springs were discovered in 1816 and a

> Given the presence of larger and more high profile towns it may appear surprising that Trowbridge is Wiltshire's county town. The reason is communications. A notoriously difficult county to negotiate, Trowbridge was the easiest to reach by rail.

pump room, baths and promenades were developed, along with crescents of houses, but the experiment ultimately failed.

Sitting on a ridge by the insignificant River Bliss, Trowbridge's position proved attractive to both Iron Age and, later on, Roman settlers, although permanent building is thought to date back to only the seventh century. By 1086 it still had only around 200 inhabitants and it passed to the de Bohun family from Edward of Salisbury as part of his daughter's dowry.

Humphrey de Bohun quickly built a motte and bailey castle which was also tested in the civil war between Stephen and Matilda, proving strong enough to resist an attack from the former. Growth followed the granting of a market charter in 1200 and within 100 years the castle had been abandoned, although it had survived long enough for its outline to define the shape of the town. The town expanded rapidly, with plots made available for tradesmen as early as the thirteenth century, with the cloth industry growing at around the same time. As Trowbridge grew, endowments in public works flowed out from the ensuing profits. The town adapted well, embracing first machinery and then steam, using its position on the canal to 'import' coal, which gave a more predictable source of power than the Bliss. By 1820 the town had fifteen factories, was nicknamed 'the Manchester of the west', and was only overtaken in size by Salisbury in 1871.

Textiles remained central to the town's economy until 1982, when the last factory closed, but the transition towards other sources of income was a smooth one, with engineering and bedmaking,

> Such was the importance of Bradford's bridge that when it needed funds for repairs in 1400 no lesser authority than the Pope appealed for the faithful to empty their pockets.

amongst others, taking up the slack. It was also around this time that Trowbridge became an administrative centre.

More evidence of Roman settlement exists for Bradford, which owes its name less to its northern namesake than to a corruption of 'Broad Ford' in acknowledgement to its position on the Avon. Recent excavations have revealed high-status Roman archaeology, including an intricate mosaic.

A sturdy stone bridge over the river was built in Norman times which still exists today, the upstream half of a passageway extended in the early 1900s. The river also acts as a divide between the old and new towns.

The Saxons were also busy in Bradford. St Adhelm founded a monastery there in the seventh century; this was subsequently destroyed by the Danes but was probably responsible for the founding of the current church of St Lawrence. The estate passed to Shaftesbury Abbey in 1001, given by King Ethelred in atonement for the murder of his half-brother by Queen Elfrida.

Ownership remained with the Abbey after the Conquest and by the mid-thirteenth century Bradford, too, was developing its cloth industry and in the fourteenth century the Abbey ordered the building of the Tithe Barn as a place to collect the tithes, which suggests that these must have been substantial.

By the fifteenth century the cloth industry had really taken off, specialising in undyed broadcloth, and by this time many of the town's buildings were made of stone, indicating significant wealth, with further expansion of the town following for at least another three centuries.

Bradford also adapted well to the introduction of mechanisation, even though this was accompanied by some protests. By 1830 the town had thirty early factories, and as soon as it became available steam power was introduced to these. A wharf was built alongside the new canal in 1823, and the waterway was used not only for goods but also to carry passengers to Bath, Bristol and London. Decline set in by the 1830s, hastened by the collapse of the local bank. Showing some versatility, the town branched out into new industries such as rubber and for many years the town was the headquarters of the Avon Rubber Co. The last cloth mill shut in 1905 and today the town has become something of a tourist destination, its charm protected by the Bradford upon Avon Preservation Trust which has rescued many of the town's finest buildings.

Other settlements of note along this stretch include Bromham to the east of Melksham, which grew in medieval times and was bought by Sir Edward Baynton from the Crown in 1538. Baynton proceeded to build a palace that rivalled Whitehall in size, using materials salvaged from Devizes Castle and a royal manor house in Corsham. This was grand enough to entertain not only Henry VIII but also James I on no less than three occasions.

Bromham suffered from changes in the clothing industry and from the Civil War, with Bromham House burned down in May 1645. These days the area is known for its market gardening.

Also worthy of mention along this stretch are Hilperton north-east of Trowbridge, which also benefited from the cloth industry, and Holt, north of the canal, which, like Melksham, enjoyed a brief moment in the sun as a spa destination, offering a summer season to balance Bath's winter.

THE NATURAL LANDSCAPE

The River Avon makes its first appearance just after Melksham and defines the landscape from here into Bath. To the east the less prominent Semington Brook wriggles away from its source just north of Bulkington, picking up the smaller Summerham Brook along the way before crossing the canal just north of the village that bears its name and finally surrendering to the mighty Avon.

Melksham lies in the valley of the Avon with higher land to the east, notably towards Seend, which sits on the plateau of a hill. Trowbridge sits in the low-lying claylands of the Avon on a limestone ridge known as the Trowbridge Anticline which rests 50ft above the clay. Bradford, meanwhile, sits on the hill that marks the western edge of the Vale of Pewsey, enjoying a position between the Mendips, Salisbury Plain and the Cotswold Hills.

ACCESS AND TRANSPORT

ROADS

The A361 heads west out of Devizes, with the A342 striking a path out towards Chippenham in the north. The former links Devizes with Trowbridge and forks outside Seend, with the A365 providing a route into Melksham. The A3102 links Melksham to a mid-way point on the A342 between Chippenham and Devizes. The A350 also passes through Melksham, taking a north/south route and intersecting with the A361 to the south outside Semington. Meanwhile, the A363 links Trowbridge to Bradford on Avon, its neighbour a couple of miles to the north-west.

There is a good network of minor roads linking the large number of smaller settlements dotted amongst these three reasonably sized towns, although the Avon begins to make its presence felt with its valley, along with those of other local streams, providing a natural barrier.

RAIL

As befits the 'three-town theme' of this section, Melksham, Trowbridge and Bradford all have their own railway station, although they are joined by Avoncliff. Trains serving all four are run by Wessex Trains (0845 6000880). The first of these has a small local service with ten trains a day, mainly heading for Swindon via Chippenham to the north and south to Trowbridge. Trowbridge, Bradford and Avoncliff all lie on one of Wessex's main lines linking Southampton and Bristol, via Bath Spa. From Bristol it is possible to connect with the South West, South Wales and London.

Of the four stations Avoncliff's is probably the most memorable, sitting on the side of the Avon Valley near the aqueduct with which it shares its name. For more detailed information contact National Train Enquiries on 08457 484950 or www.nationalrail.co.uk.

BUSES

The following list sets out the main bus services on this section although it is advisable to check before using them as some buses only run on certain days and others may have been withdrawn since publication of this Guide. It is also worth checking for more local services, especially within the more major towns.

- 33 – *Devizes to Chippenham via Bromham and Rowde (APL)*
- 37 – *Bradford on Avon to Chippenham via Holt and Melksham (Bodmans)*
- 38 – *Bradford on Avon to Trowbridge via Holt and Melksham (Bodmans)*
- 39 – *Bradford on Avon to Devizes via Holt, Shaw,*

Semington and Seend (Bodmans)
- 49 – *Trowbridge to Swindon via Hilperton and Seend (Stagecoach)*
- 64 – *Hilperton to Bath via Bradford, Thurleigh and Winsleys (Beeline). Fridays only*
- 77 – *Trowbridge to Devizes via Hilperton via Keevil and Bulkington (Badgerline)*
- 94 – *Trowbridge to Bath via Westwood (Badgerline)*
- 96 – *Bradford on Avon to*

Trowbridge via Westwood (Bodmans)
- 234 – *Frome to Chippenham via Trowbridge, Hilperton, Semington and Melksham (Badgerline)*
- 236 – *Hilperton to Trowbridge (Badgerline)*
- 237 – *Trowbridge to Melksham via Holt (Badgerline)*
- 265 – *Melksham to Bath via Semington, Trowbridge, Bradford (Pickford)*

In addition, the X4 Bath to Salisbury express passes through a number of the destinations in this section, as does the X5 Bath to Warminster route. The 402 Express from Frome to London stops at Trowbridge and Melksham. In addition, the X34 Frome to Chippenham Express links Trowbridge, Semington and Melksham.

Contact details for bus operators in this area are listed below, although Traveline (www.traveline.org.uk) on 0870 6082608 can give details of specific services between 7 a.m. and 10 p.m.:

- APL, Malmesbury (01666 577774)
- Beeline, Warminster (01985 213503)
- Badgerline (First Somerset and Avon), Weston super Mare (08456 064446)
- Bodmans Coaches, Worton (01380 722393)
- Pickford, Chippenham (01249 444444)
- Stagecoach, Swindon (01793 522243)

TAXIS
The following list gives a selection of taxi operators in this section:

- A&D Taxis, Trowbridge (01225 751332)
- A&P Taxis, Melksham (01225 706133)
- Alpha Taxis, Trowbridge (01225 753218)
- Ashley Cabs, Bradford on Avon (01225 861111)
- Andy's Taxis, Melksham (01225 704426)
- Avon Taxis, Melksham (01225 345075)
- Beta Taxis, Trowbridge
- (01373 822986)
- City Cars, Melksham (01225 700038)
- First County Cars, Trowbridge (01225 352173)
- Millwood Travel, Bradford on Avon (01225 868851)
- Paul's Freephone Taxi, Melksham (0808 0500400)
- Oz Cabs, Trowbridge (01225 753000)
- R. Reeves, Rowde (01380 725072)

SECTION E

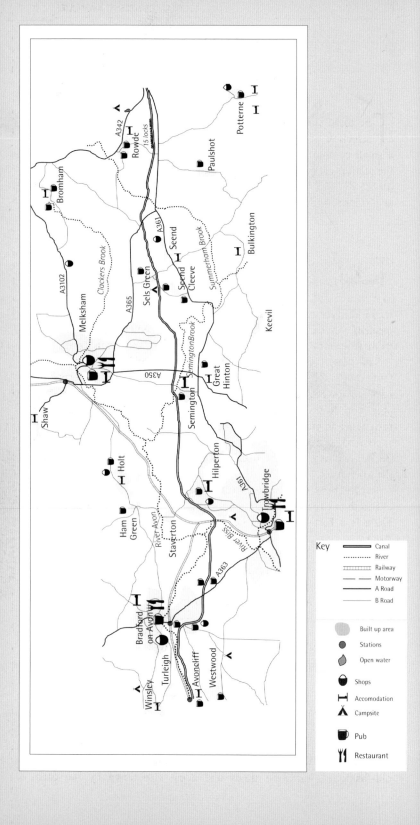

BASICS

INTRODUCTION

The three market towns that dominate this s
selection of options to meet basic needs. B.
a small community hospital (01225 862975) and ___e in
the station car park, whilst Melksham (01225 7010\ ...ıd Trowbridge
(01225 752558) also each have community hospitals. None of these has
an Accident and Emergency.

SHOPPING

There is no shortage of places to stock up along this stretch, with each
of the towns along it all offering their own mix of shops. All seem
to have avoided the attentions of the large international chains, and thus
retain much of their traditional market-town feel, with a variety of independent stores and the odd boutique or niche outlet scattered amongst
them. A few of the surrounding villages also have their own stores.

Sandridge Farm, near Bromham, is famous for its bacon and has a
farm shop, with a butcher in Bromham itself. Seend and Potterne both
have village stores, although Melksham acts as the next major shopping stop. Not a particularly inspiring centre, the Melksham shopping
experience is probably best described as 'basic'. There is a Sainsbury's
supermarket in the heart of the town and a Somerfield and Co-op on
the edge, along with the usual banks, pharmacies and off-licences in
the town itself.

The feel here is best summed up by the Avon Place centre, a collection
of less than exciting outlets, and the Old Stable second-hand emporium.
There is a Farmers' Market here, though, every second Friday of the
month.

Holt has the Holt Superstore and a post office, but the next main
centre is Trowbridge. Silver Street leading into Market Street is the main
drag here, although the bigger shops actually sit in the pedestrianised
Fore Street, the historic centre of the town. There is also the Shires Mall,
as well as more shops in Castle Street. As has become the modern way,
most food shopping seems to have migrated to a large edge of town
Tesco's. There is also a Lidl nearer to the canal, a brisk walk from the
Hilperton Marina, as well as a Farmers' Market every fourth Friday
monthly.

The shops in Bradford on Avon are more accessible from the canal,
with the tempting Crusty Bloomers bakery a sign of things to come.
That said, they remain a good 10 minutes' walk away. As well as a
selection of natural and fine food shops, there is also a cheese specialist
here and a 'real meat' butcher. There are art studios also, as well as good
old-fashioned hardware shops and cycle hire down by the canal.

as a weekly open market and it should come as no sur-
...osts regular antiques markets and craft fairs. The Farmers'
...ere is every third Thursday at Westbury Gardens.

EATING AND DRINKING

This is a section well blessed with pubs, both in the three main towns and in the surrounding villages, most of which have at least one watering hole. The following lists offer a selection from each:

MELKSHAM
- The Barge Inn (01380 828230)
- The Bear (01225 702901)
- The Parson's Nose (01225 702947)
- The Somerset Arms (01380 870067)

TROWBRIDGE AREA
- Black Swan, Trowbridge (01225 755847)
- The Court House, Trowbridge (01225 754016)
- The Dursley Arms, Trowbridge (01225 752089)
- The Greyhound, Trowbridge (01225 752271)
- The Kings Arms, Hilperton (01225 755168) – *a short walk from Bridge No.166*
- The Kings Arms, Trowbridge (01225 751310)
- Lion and Fiddle, Hilperton (01225 782487)
- Old Bear Inn, Staverton (01225 782487)
- The White Swan, Trowbridge (01225 753723)

BRADFORD ON AVON
- The Barge Inn (01225 863403)
- The Bear (01225 866632)
- Bunch of Grapes (01225 863877)
- The Canal Tavern (01225 867426) – *canalside*
- The Dandy Lion (01225 863433)
- The Kings Arms (01225 755168) – *Hilperton Wharf*
- Lock Inn (01225 868068)
- The Mill House (01225 862004)
- The Riverside Inn (01225 863526)
- Three Horseshoes (01225 865876)

SURROUNDING VILLAGES
- Cross Keys, Rowde (01380 722368)
- George and Dragon, Rowde (01380 723053)
- Greyhound, Bromham (01380 850241)
- Oliver Cromwell, Bromham (01380 850293) – *on the Rowde Road*
- George and Dragon, Potterne (01380 722139)
- Raven, Paulshot (01380 828271)

- The Barge Inn, Seend (01380 828230)
- Bell Inn, Seend (01380 828338)
- The Brewery Inn, Seend Cleeve (01380 828463)
- Three Magpies, Sells Green (01380 828389)
- Toll Gate, Holt (01225 782326)
- Old Ham Tree, Ham Green (01225 782581)
- The New Inn, Westwood (01225 863123)
- Cross Guns, Avoncliff (01225 862335)

The high density of towns also lends itself to a choice of places to eat, although the range of restaurants can vary with the most select establishments gravitating towards Bradford. Again, the following lists offer a selection of what is available:

MELKSHAM
- Conigre Farm Restaurant (01225 702229)
- The Fisheries (01225 703406) – *fish and chips*
- Lee's Palace (01225 793388) – *Chinese takeaway*
- The Melksham Tandoori (01225 705242) – *Indian*

TROWBRIDGE
- The Bejing Palace (01225 781188) – *Chinese*
- The Codfather (01225 774235) – *fish and chips*
- Dinos (01225 760600) – *Italian takeaway*
- Manyee (01225 752302) – *Chinese takeaway*
- The Royal Spice (01225 766799) – *Indian takeaway*
- Trail of Spice (01225 776591) – *Indian*

BRADFORD ON AVON
- Chinatown (01225 862071) – *Chinese takeaway*
- Feng Shui (01225 866628) – *Chinese*
- The Georgian Lodge (01225 862268) – *traditional*
- Le Mange Tout (01225 863111) – *French*
- The Maharaja (01225 866424) – *Indian close to the canal*
- Pizza Amici (01225 863661) – *Italian*
- Rialto (01225 862123) – *Italian*
- The Thai Barn (01225 866443) – *Thai*

This is also a good section to linger in if you like your afternoon tea. The following list offers a selection of local cafés and snack places:

- www.tato.co.uk, Melksham (01225 404555) – *snack bar*
- The Cornerstone Coffee Shop, Melksham (01225 792000)
- Bridge Tea Rooms, Bradford on Avon (01225 865537)
- The Cottage Café, Bradford on Avon (01225 867444) – *organic and fair trade café with internet access*

SECTION E

- The Lock Inn Cafe, Bradford on Avon (01225 868068) – *canalside café*
- The Scribbling Horse, Bradford on Avon (01225 862495) – *tea shop*
- Teazels Tea Rooms, Bradford on Avon (01225 868123)
- The Mad Hatter Tearoom, Avoncliff (01225 868123)

The Kennet & Avon Canal Trust also has a tearoom at the wharf in Bradford which also sells souvenirs (01225 868683).

SLEEPING

Again, the concentration of large market towns means there is no shortage of choice when it comes to finding somewhere to stay, although there is also plenty of choice away from the towns. The following list offers a snapshot only of what is available:

HOTELS

- Lamb Inn on The Strand, Seend (01380 870815)
- The Tipsy Toad, Bulkington (01380 828741)
- The Linnet, Great Hinton (01380 870354)
- Conigre Farm Hotel, Melksham (01225 702229)
- The Kings Arms Hotel, Melksham (01225 707272)
- The Shaw Country Hotel, Shaw (01225 702836)
- Hilbury Court Hotel, Hilperton (01225 752949)
- Fieldways Hotel and Health Club, Trowbridge (01225 768336)
- The Old Manor Hotel, Trowbridge (01225 777393)
- The Polebarn Hotel, Trowbridge (01225 754006)
- Leigh Park Hotel, Bradford on Avon (01225 864885) – *Best Western*
- The Swan Hotel, Bradford on Avon (01225 868686) – *sixteenth-century town centre hotel*
- Widbrook Grange, Bradford on Avon (01225 864750) – *small hotel set in a Georgian country house*
- Woolley Grange Hotel, Bradford on Avon (01225 864705) – *small country house*

BED AND BREAKFAST/GUEST HOUSES

- Brookside, Rowde (01380 726394)
- Paddock House, Bromham (01380 850970)
- Yew Tree Cottage, Bromham (01380 850515)
- Blounts Court Farm, Potterne (01380 727180)
- Frogsleap, Potterne
- (01380 727761)
- The Old Manor House B&B, Semington (01380 870450)
- The Bridge House B&B, Semington (01225 703281)
- The Somerset Arms, Semington (01380 870067) – *a short walk up from Bridge No.160*
- The Tollgate, Holt

(01225 782326)
- The Lion and Fiddle, Hilperton (01225 776392)
- Paxcroft Cottages, Hilperton (01225 765838)
- Biss Barn, Trowbridge (01225 710372)
- The Barge Inn, Bradford on Avon (01225 863403)
- Beeches Farmhouse, Bradford on Avon (0870 478 6358)
- Bradford Old Windmill, Bradford on Avon (01225 866842) – *romantic ex-windmill*
- Great Ashley Farm, Bradford on Avon (01225 864563)
- Locks, Bradford on Avon (01225 863358) – *canalside B&B*
- Burghope Manor, Winsley (01225 723557)
- Avonvilla B&B, Avoncliff (01225 863867)

CAMPING

Campers are well catered for on this stretch with a particular concentration of sites around Devizes and the canal. The main sites include:

- Church Farm, Winsley (01225 722246) – *small farm-based site*
- Lakeside, Rowde (01380 722767)
- Lower Foxhangers, Devizes (01380 828254) – *B&B and camping at the foot of the Caen Hill flight*
- Longscroft Caravan and Camping, Trowbridge (01225 765400) – *half a mile from the canal*
- Sells Green, Devizes (01380 828839) – *large camping and caravanning club site*
- Stowford Manor Farm, Trowbridge (01225 752253) – *small site amongst medieval farm*
- Three Magpies, Devizes (01380 828389) – *next to a pub and near to the canal*

The nearest camping supplies outlets in this section are:
- Coyote Camping and Outdoor Leisure, Melksham (01225 899388)
- BCH Camping and Leisure, Trowbridge (01225 764977)
- Millets, Trowbridge (01225 762871)

The wharf at Bradford on Avon.

SECTION E

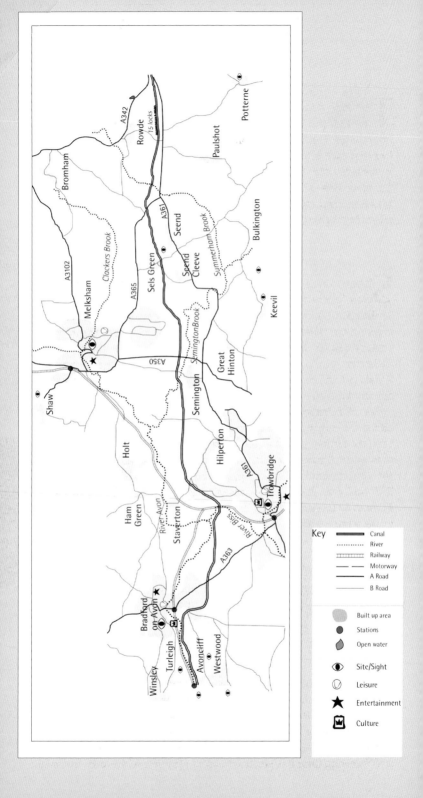

SEEING AND DOING

INTRODUCTION

The three towns of Trowbridge (01225 710535), Melksham (01225 707424) and Bradford (01225 865797) each have their own Tourist Information Centres (see 'Learn More and Links'), a reflection of the fact that each offers its own mix of places to see and go to. Trowbridge is probably the most cosmopolitan of the three, whilst Bradford is the more impressive when it comes to sights. Many of the villages in between remain worth a visit though, with some of the more significant sights highlighted here.

SIGHTS

Slightly out of the way, Potterne is worth seeing as it contains more than its fair share of history for such a small place. The approach to the centre is dramatic and leads to a short run of half-timbered cottages on the main street. The village church dates back to the thirteenth century and its size is accounted for by the fact that the Bishops of Salisbury once owned much of the surrounding land and even had a palace here in the Middle Ages. Inside, the church has an eighth-century font from the church's predecessor.

East of Potterne lies the totally unexpected Keevil Airfield. Constructed during the early days of the Second World War as an Operational Training Unit, the airfield played a significant part in the D-Day landings and the subsequent Armheim operations. Although the original plan was to return the requisitioned land back to those who had farmed it before the war, the RAF held onto it due to its convenience for nearby Salisbury Plain. The Norman St Leonard's church in Keevil is also worth a visit, with decorated wooden tracery above its tie beams a particular feature.

Seend on the canal is significant for being the site of a Victorian ironworks and evidence of this past are visible in the village, including the works manager's house (the appropriately named Ferrum Lodge) and remains of the broadgauge railway that carried the pig iron and coal between the works and the local station.

John Fowler of Melksham was the inventor of the first steam plough and his sister, Rachel, a great Quaker, became a benefactress to the town and was responsible for the Town Hall.

Melksham to the north is a sleepy market town with evidence of a more dynamic past, including cloth weaving and, for a while, a prominent position on the Wilts & Berks Canal, the route of which it is still possible to pick out. The names of Rope Walk and Wharf Court also betray this past.

The Tourist Information Office in Melksham sells two short town trails and following these it is possible to take in features of the town that might otherwise be missed. Highlights include an old bread oven, various bas reliefs and the history behind otherwise unprepossessing buildings. The older part of Melksham gravitates towards the church and there is a pleasant stroll to be had along Church Walk along the back of the town; look out especially for No.16 which has a vine growing over its lintel. More obvious attractions in Melksham include the Town Hall and Market Place, along with some almshouses. Melksham also has a riverside walk if you want to get away from the traffic.

Although only around 100 years old, the spire of Christ Church, Shaw, to the east of Melksham, is worth stopping by to see. Ornate with gargoyles, the church dominates the side of the road and seems out of proportion to its surroundings.

Being the county town has undoubtedly helped maintain Trowbridge's importance. The town can claim to have been an industrial centre as early as the fourteenth century, although much of the cloth work being carried out would have taken place in people's homes rather than large factories. Plenty of examples of this heritage remain today, including weaver's homes and workshops as well as some of the larger mills that followed. The best of these can be seen by following an industrial trail in a booklet available at the Tourist Information Office. The office also offers a town trail, although sites on this also have blue plaques with more information on them.

Highlights of this tour include the 'Blind House', a local name for a gaol which refers to the lack of windows and The Parade, a collection of clothier's houses subsequently used as the headquarters of Usher's Brewery. Look out also for Polebarn House and the magnificent Town Hall. A county town, Trowbridge boasts both a Town and a County Hall.

> Polebarn House in Polebarn Road was built in 1789 by the minister John Clark and had not only a miniature country house garden with a grotto, lake and gazebo but also a domed observatory on the roof. It is now a hotel.

Trowbridge also houses Trowbridge Museum (01225 751339) which gives more background on the town's past, in particular, but not exclusively, its links with the cloth industry. Trowbridge was also the birthplace of Isaac Pitman and another town trail starts at the museum and locates all the main sites associated with this man, the inventor of phonography. Pitman was a great Victorian thinker, remembered for the system of shorthand that bears his name based upon the sounds of words. A permanent display to his life is housed in the museum. Finally, in Trowbridge, there is the Community Sensory Garden at the rear of the Town Hall

Bradford looks like the sort of place with much to offer and does not disappoint. Before heading up the hill start by going against the flow and pass over the bridge by the lock, heading left and then right. Through a gap in the houses it is possible to gain a good appreciation of how the town clings to the side of the hill and spreads out along it, which will make it easier to understand the geography of the town when you do head into it. The Tourist Information Office is on the left before the bridge, itself a main attraction. This dates back to the thirteenth century

Half-timbered houses at Potterne.

and spans the Avon, giving the town its suffix, although the current stone version dates back to the seventeenth century. Look out for the Bradford Gudgeon weathervane on the bridge, along with the small building that was once the town gaol.

On the other side of the road from the Tourist Information Centre, and easy to miss, is 'Millie' by John Willats, who won a national competition organised by the council. The sculpture represents aspects of the three millennia in the town, with Millie herself representing a mill girl.

On the subject of mills, the view on returning to the bridge is also worth taking in as it encompasses old weaver's cottages and nineteenth-century cloth mills. A riverside walk takes you past some of these from the other side of the bridge. The town itself is worth a wander. Lacking a true heart, although this is part of the town's charm, it is easy to get lost and while away the odd hour browsing the interesting collection of shops.

Another must-see in Bradford is the Tithe Barn, back towards the canal, which was built in the early fourteenth century on land belonging to the Abbey of Shaftesbury. This important medieval building is now part of a small complex which includes Barton Farmhouse and a Granary, with the latter restored and operated as a shop. The barn itself is a cruck and its 16ft-long roof has to be seen to be believed.

Finally in Bradford look out for the Saxon church of St Lawrence, one of many historic churches in the town. Built in the early eleventh century for the nuns of Shaftesbury, it is still in use today. Tall and narrow with small windows, the church is typical of its time. Before leaving, locate the pair of angels found in 1855 on the east wall of the nave.

To the east of Bradford, sandwiched between the river and the canal, is the Barton Farm Country Park, a 36-acre recreational area with picnic tables and wildlife spots. A walk through the Park takes you from the Tithe Barn to the Avoncliff Aqueduct in around 45 minutes. This magnificent John Rennie structure has been recently restored, and is a key feature of the rejuvenated canal.

Westwood Manor (01225 863374), south-west of Bradford, is a National Trust house boasting Jacobean and Gothic plasterwork and windows. There is also an attractive topiary garden here. Also nearby, east of Westwood, is Ilford Manor (01225 863146), the home of architect and landscape gardener Harold A. Peto in the early part of the twentieth century. As might be expected, the main feature is the romantic hillside garden with its terraces, sculptures and views.

CULTURE AND ENTERTAINMENT

Melksham has the Christie Miller Sports Centre (01225 702826) which has ten-pin bowling, squash courts, indoor bowls and a 9-hole golf course. In addition, Melksham has the Wiltshire School of Gymnastics (01225 793402) specialising in gymnastics and trampolining and the Blue Pool (01225 703525), a health and leisure facility with a 33m pool and a gym.

Trowbridge has the Castle Place Leisure Centre (01225 762711), focusing on gym work, and its own Sports Centre (01225 764342) with a 25m indoor swimming pool as well as a sports hall, squash courts and a diving pit. This is sited next to the large open area of Trowbridge Park, known locally as the 'People's Park' which as well as all-weather floodlit tennis courts has a bowling green and a children's play area. The Park also hosts musical events during the year along with the West Wilts Show. Bradford, meanwhile, has a 25m pool near the heart of the town (01225 862970) which also has a health suite with sauna and solarium.

When it comes to the arts, the main venue is in Trowbridge which has the Arc Theatre (01225 756376) in the grounds of the college, specialising in innovative theatre and dance. Nightlife is similarly thin on the ground. If it is live music you are after it is best to head for the pubs in Trowbridge, notably the Black Swan, Greyhound and Dursley Arms (see 'Basics'). Terry's Club on Hill Street (01225 351100) is also worth checking out.

Bradford, on the other hand, has its own jazz club (01225 400959) and the Wiltshire Music Centre, where you might hear anything from Classical guitar to Baroque. There is also jazz most Mondays at the George Inn, Wooley Street (01225 865650).

The tower of Christ Church, Shaw.

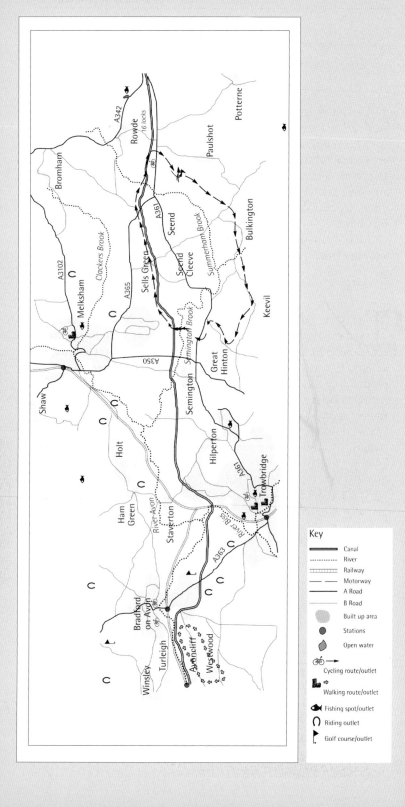

Key

▬▬▬	Canal
········	River
▥▥▥▥	Railway
─ ─ ─	Motorway
▬▬▬	A Road
───	B Road
	Built up area
●	Stations
◗	Open water
🚲→	Cycling route/outlet
👢⇨	Walking route/outlet
🐟	Fishing spot/outlet
∩	Riding outlet
⚑	Golf course/outlet

SAMPLING

INTRODUCTION

On one level quite a populated section it is also quite easy to feel a long way from anywhere along here, with wide rural stretches north and south of the towpath punctuated by only the occasional village either side of the Trowbridge/Melksham axis. The Avon comes alongside the route just west of Melksham, eventually making contact with the canal just after Trowbridge. Bradford offers a dramatic end point just before the river disappears into woodland.

The OS Explorer Map covering this stretch is No.156, Chippenham and Bradford on Avon.

WALKING

The White Horse Trail joins up with the towpath just east of Devizes and heads south from it at the base of the Caen Hill flight, heading off towards Bulkington. Otherwise, the main formal route along this section is the Macmillan Way which passes north–south through Bradford on Avon. The towpath acts as a magnet for other local footpaths, however, with most of the villages featured here linked by ancient routes, most of which are well signposted.

Walk E focuses on the western edge of the section and combines the Avoncliff Aqueduct with a chance to sample views of Bradford on Avon.

SECTION E WALK
From Bradford and Back via the Westwoods and Avoncliff

Description:	*A relatively short walk with a couple of inclines offering good views and access to the Avoncliff Aqueduct*
Distance:	*4 miles*
Duration:	*1½hrs*
Staring point:	*Grid Reference 825611, OS Explorer 156*
Nearest refreshment:	*The New Inn, Westwood*

From the station car park pass under the railway bridge by the river. Follow this into the Country Park, passing to the right of the Tithe Barn. Head up some steps to the towpath and then left to the Canal Tavern. Go right at the road and over the canal bridge, turning right at Canal Bridge House and up Jones Hill. On reaching a stile on your left, cross and head to the right of an old ventilation shaft in the field ahead. On reaching a hedge cross a stile, keep the hedge on your right and go over another stile.

Pass through a gap in the hedge and over another stile with a radio mast to your right. Head half left and pass over a stone stile halfway along the hedge. Turn right and over another stile, heading for the corner of the field. Go over two more stiles and cross the field diagonally, heading towards the village via a stile in the corner of the field. Pass over a pair of stiles and to the right of some bungalows, bringing you to the pub. Follow the road opposite Westwood Manor, passing the car park on your left, and enter the churchyard.

Follow the path until it heads right, where you go straight ahead. Pass over fields to a lane in the corner, at the end of which you need to go down some steps to a road. Turn left then right by the Baptist Chapel. Enter a field via a kissing gate, following the hedge to another gate. Turn right here and pass behind some houses and follow the road to Upper Westwood. Follow the footpath downhill to Avoncliff and, on reaching the Aqueduct, pick up the towpath which leads you back to Bradford and your starting point.

Walking equipment outlets along this section include:
- BCH Camping and Leisure, Trowbridge (01225 764977)
- Coyote Camping and Leisure, Melksham (01225 899388)
- Millets, Trowbridge (01225 762871)

CYCLING

National Cycle Route 4 continues to favour the towpath along this section, but also takes time to encompass Melksham and Bradford on Avon. Most of the minor roads lie to the south of the canal.

A route which allows you to sample some of this section on two wheels starts at the camp site at Lower Foxhangers Farm and follows the White Horse Trail over the A361 and south along Broadway Lane to Townsend, where it briefly picks up a road before heading west to Bulkington.

Once in the village pick up the road and head west, through Keevil to a crossroads where you head north (right) through Great Hinton to Horseshoe Farm. Pass briefly along the A361 again, heading left, and pick up the first road on the right. This dog-legs to the left and picks up a track on the right heading down to Seend Park Farm. Here you pick up the towpath and head east (right) for 3 miles back to your starting point – a total distance of around 14 miles.

Cycle outlets along this section include:
- The Bike Shop, Bradford on Avon (01225 868068) – *by the lock*
- TT Cycles, Bradford on Avon (01225 867187)
- Palmers, Trowbridge (01225 777117)
- Melksham Cycle Centre, Melksham (01225 709878)

Bradford on Avon clinging to the hillside.

RIDING

There is good riding to be had along parts of the White Horse Trail, including Towmead Lane west of Bulkington and Broadway Lane south of Foxhangers. There are also a number of bridleways north of the A365, east of Melksham, and tracks between Hilperton and Semington. Seend and Seend Cleeve also have paths.

Horse-riding establishments and outlets along this section include:
- Staverton Farm Livery, Staverton (01225 782327)
- Hill View Riding Stables, Holt (01225 783217)
- rideyourbest.com, Seend (01380 828319)
- West Wilts Equestrian Centre, Trowbridge (01225 783220)
- RD Fry, Bradford on Avon (01225 863361)
- Widbrook Arabian Stud & Equestrian Centre (01225 862608)
- Ellbridge Stables, Bradford on Avon (01225 864664)
- Church Farm Livery, Bradford on Avon (01225 858583)

FISHING

Devizes AA (01380 860479) continues to control the canal west of Devizes as far as Semington Bridge by the junction with the old Wilts & Berks Canal, with a large head of tench and decent-sized carp. Fishing is not allowed through the Caen Hill flight, but just above it is a good area for pike. Otherwise, contact either the Melksham AA (01225 705036) for details of canal fishing elsewhere on this section or Bradford on Avon AA which controls the section between Semington Bridge to Avoncliff Aqueduct and between Bradford Lock and Winsley Bridge.

Fishing is also possible at Rowde Lake, attached to the camp site there, Orchard Farm, just west of Melksham, a small lake with good carp, bream and chub, and Leechpool Farm, also near Melksham, where

Trowbridge Town Hall and Market Street.

there are some decent-sized carp. Finally, there is Rood Ashton, a carp lake outside Trowbridge.

Trout fishing is also possible at Mill Farm Trout Lakes near Worton, south-west of Potterne (01380 813138).

Outlets selling fishing supplies along this stretch include:
• Avon Angling, Melksham (01225 702219)
• West's Tackle, Trowbridge (01225 755472)
• Wiltshire Angling, Trowbridge (01225 763835)

OTHER

Although Bradford on Avon's course (01225 868268) is the only full golf course on this section, there are also a couple of other shorter ones worth visiting:

• Cumberwell Park Golf Club, Bradford on Avon (01225 863322) – *27-hole course broken down into three sets of 9 holes covering parkland,* *woodland and lakeland respectively*
• Whitley Golf Course, Melksham (01255 790099) – *9 holes, 2,200 yards*

SECTION F

AVONCLIFF TO BATH

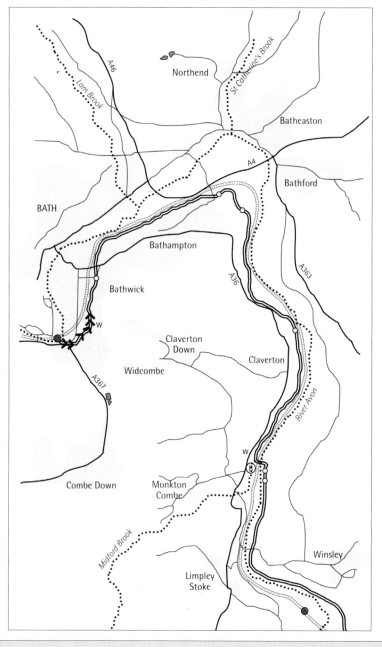

Northend

St Catherine's Brook

Batheaston

A46

Lam Brook

A4

Bathford

BATH

Bathampton

A363

A36

Bathwick

W

Claverton
Down

Claverton

Widcombe

A367

River Avon

Combe Down

Monkton
Combe

W
B

Winsley

Midford Brook

Limpley
Stoke

Key

══════ Canal		Built up area	⭕ Turning point
·········· River		Stations	⋀ Lock
▥▥▥▥ Railway		Open water	Ⓑ Boatyard
─ ─ ─ Motorway			W Waterpoint
─── A Road			
─── B Road			

SHAPERS

THE CANAL ON THIS STRETCH

KEY FACTS

LENGTH: 9 miles

BOATYARDS: 1
   Somerset Coal Canal

WATERPOINTS: 2
   Dundas Wharf
   Bathwick

TURNING POINTS: 6
   Conkwell Wood
   Dundas Wharf
   Claverton
   Bathampton
   Bathampton Bridge
   Bathwick
   NB: Turning is also possible in the Avon after Bath Bottom Lock

LOCKS: 6
   Bath Top Lock (9ft)
   Pulteney Lock (9ft 5in)
   Abbey View Lock (9ft)
   Wash House Lock (8ft 6in)
   Bath Deep Lock (19ft 5in)
   Bath Bottom Lock (9ft 3in)

From its earliest stages, this section is dominated by views over the Avon Valley and the Mendips. Although the glory that is Bath is the ultimate prize, there is plenty to admire along the way, including an aqueduct, some magnificent scenery and the deep Bath Locks flight.

There is another long run of mooring after the Avoncliff Aqueduct and this marks a trend from here onwards, making it difficult for boats to maintain a regular speed. This is a temptation easily resisted, however, as the views along this stretch are amongst the best anywhere on the canal system, even if they are often hidden by trees. High hills to the right and views out to the Avon Valley on the left, along with a tranquil tree-lined towpath, make this a charming walk in any season.

Bridges are few and far between and the canal's route is at times as straight as a die, its sides being hard-lined and pock-marked with regular wooden duck-ramps. A long sweep to the right before Limpley Stoke Bridge pulls the canal north, following the course of the Avon, which it crosses over again at the Dundas Aqueduct.

This is, if anything, more spectacular than the Avoncliff, with excellent views over the valley, although the railway scratches something of a scar across it and the occasional express train can shatter the silence. This is also the site of the junction of the old Somerset Coal Canal, a short section of which to the left is occupied by a boatyard, with a watering point and DIY pump put straight ahead.

> The Somerset Coal Canal Act was passed in 1794 in order to create an easier way to transport coal into the heart of Bath. By the 1820s it was carrying over 100,000 tons of the black stuff a year, although within fifty years it was victim to competition from the railways.

The canal now continues relentlessly northward. A run of long-term mooring ends with some of the 48-hour variety near Bridge No.180, after which the canal narrows with reeds, bulrushes and bamboo all encroaching the bank-side, so that the canal becomes almost single file in places.

After Bathampton Swing Bridge the ground rises dramatically to the left and the canal appears to hang on for dear life to the hillside, with a steep drop to the right. Yet more mooring follows, with the outskirts of Bath at last beginning to show themselves. A series of canalside cottages at Bathampton make for a pretty scene after which there is a final long stretch before Bath itself. The honey-coloured terraces of that city slowly begin to cluster on the hillsides on the right and some large Georgian edifices appear much closer to hand on the left.

Soon after that stone is incorporated into the bridges, although the footbridges that announce your arrival in Bath proper are of iron and were erected over 200 years ago. One of these, Sydney Gardens Footbridge (No.186), presages the magnificent Cleveland House Tunnel, which in turn comes before the six Bath Locks, although the last but one of these is, in fact, a double lock in terms of depth, with one member of the flight falling victim to a road scheme some time ago. Reputedly either the deepest or second deepest on the system, with a drop just short of 20ft, this is a real experience for boaters and one probably best done in company.

On exiting the last of the locks it is necessary to fork to the left to follow the route of the canal (although here you are in fact on the Avon), with boaters having to sound their horn as a warning to oncoming traffic. Following this direction will eventually take you to Bristol, although after a while the water becomes tidal. If possible, it is worth turning right, however, where there are some of the best moorings available anywhere in terms of their view, just below Bath Abbey and Pulteney Bridge. It may come as something of a shock to discover that a fee is levied here, although payment at the sports centre does carry with it access to the showers and facilities there.

PRINCIPAL TOWNS AND VILLAGES ALONG THIS STRETCH

BATH

Bath exerts an overpowering presence on the area, with local villages even incorporating its name in theirs. The distinctive honey-coloured stone dominates, and the city features a number of set pieces, each equally impressive. Understandably, the city is a designated UNESCO World Heritage Site.

BATHEASTON

Defiantly separate from Bath, a fact that residents have celebrated by painting many of the properties rather than leaving the Bath stone bare.

BATHFORD

An extensive village spread out over a hill, which has expanded significantly in recent years, not always elegantly.

BATHAMPTON

A pretty village with a pub sitting right by the side of the canal next to a bridge, with more modern housing rising up on a slope to the south.

BATHWICK

A magnificent area on the outskirts of Bath leading up to the university sitting on a steep hill, affording excellent views out towards the city.

CLAVERTON

A small, pretty village tucked away off the A36 with an elegant Manor House at its centre.

CLAVERTON DOWN

A small community that keeps itself to itself just south of the university and Bathwick Down.

COMBE DOWN

A village in two parts with the older part sitting off the main road whilst the newer section hosts government buildings and local services as well as the hospital.

LIMPLEY STOKE

Clinging to the side of the Avon Valley, with subsequent excellent views to match, Limpley Stoke is something of a warren of narrow streets bordered by high stone walls.

MONKTON COMBE

A large independent school sits at the heart of this fairly typical village.

NORTHEND
An adjunct to Batheaston lying, as its name suggests, to the north.

WIDCOMBE
Another separate location on the outskirts of Bath sitting on the junction of the canal with the River Avon.

WINSLEY
A scattered village comprising mostly older housing with a single pub.

HISTORY

The Romans and the Georgians left their marks on Bath, but the city's history goes back much further than that. Bath owes its name to the Bladud, the oldest son of Celtic King Lud. A leper, Bladud had been exiled to Swainswick, a village outside Bath, to work as a swineherd.

The legend goes that he noticed his pigs were cured of scurvy when they wallowed in the warm, hot mud thereabouts fed by a local stream. When he waded into the mud himself, his leprosy was cured. In gratitude, he built a temple dedicated to Sul, although

> Bladud is also remembered for establishing the first universities in England and for being the father of King Lear.

he met his end jumping off the top of it, but not before he had time to become king in his own right.

Bladud's discovery did not herald a building boom, however, as major development did not follow for a further 1,000 years. Rather, the Celts preferred to protect the spring, which was shadowed by an oak grove and five hillforts. The Celts believed that the spring was a gateway to the Underworld through which deities and ancestors could be reached.

The spring that has been Bath's fortune was well established, therefore, by the time the Romans arrived in AD443. In their usual fashion, the Romans rolled the local Gods up into their own and re-branded them, in this case dedicating the spring to Sulis Minerva, although they retained

> Sul was Goddess of arcane prophecy, her qualities tempered by those of Minerva, who was altogether more cultured and centred around the arts and sciences.

the belief that the spring represented some kind of portal to another world.

The Roman city was, like Rome, said to be based on seven hills, with one or more of these based around the Batheaston area. There is evidence that Batheaston itself has been occupied since Neolithic times and Little Solsbury had an Iron Age fort. Equally, Bathampton has earth works dating back to around the same time.

It was the Roman investment in Bath that was to have a transforming effect on the area, however, with the Romans making early (not altogether successful) attempts to quarry the famous Bathampton stone that dominates the skyline today.

The Roman Baths remain the centrepiece of the modern tourism industry in Bath and, although their history is covered extensively elsewhere, their importance cannot be overestimated. The Roman dominance ended when Bath fell to the Saxons at the Battle of Dyrham and the baths themselves decayed into ruins, although the city's prominence as a religious centre was recognised with the establishment of a Saxon monastery in the seventh century.

As the monastery grew richer so the power of the local Saxons grew and it was here that Edgar, the first English king, was crowned in 973. It took a new wave of invaders to disrupt things again when Somerset rose up against the Normans and reaped the dividends when Bath and its monastery were subsequently destroyed.

John de Villula was a Norman doctor who became a churchman and was able to buy the ruined city for the price of 500 pounds of silver.

Many of the surrounding settlements such as Batheaston, Bathampton and Limpley Stoke feature in the Domesday Book, but they did not grow into significant centres of population. Meanwhile, Bath had attracted the attention of John de Villula, who instituted an ambitious new building plan to establish the current cathedral, although only the nave remains of the original building. De Villula was also interested in the baths and began a programme of restoration and the building of several treatment centres.

Bishop Oliver King took charge of rebuilding the church when, in 1499, he had a dream of Jacob's Ladder, with angels ascending a ladder into heaven, proclaiming, 'Let an olive establish the crown and a King restore the church', a command he took personally given his name.

In the centuries that followed the church fell into disrepair and had to wait until the early sixteenth century to be rebuilt to take the form seen today. During this time Bath was far from fashionable, with only the sick or desperate using its waters. Desperate because, as the traveller John Leland recorded, the water 'rikketh like a seething potte'.

The city had to wait a further 200 years and the arrival of the 'dandy' Beau, or Richard Nash, for the next phase of its evolution into the attraction we know today. Despite a less than distinguished past, wherein he had flunked university, the army and the law and lived as a professional gambler, it is to Nash that the city owes its revival. Nash set out making Bath the place to be seen, and in just three years raised enough money to repair the roads, a precursor to the building of some of the most exquisite buildings the country had ever seen, this time exploiting Bathampton's stone rather more successfully than the Romans had.

Of course, at the same time Nash had established himself as the de facto ruler of Bath and created the perfect environment for his social and gambling skills. His vision attracted the talents of other great names associated with the city, including the architects Robert Adams, John Wood and Thomas Baldwin.

Their legacy remains today with Pulteney Bridge, often compared to the Ponte Vecchio in Florence; the Royal Crescent; Queen Square; and Great Pulteney Street, over 1,000ft long and 100ft wide.

These days Bath trades off this history, but has a modern heart, too. The university, based by Claverton Down, attracts the young whose presence provides a contrast to the contents of many of the coaches who visit the city every day. Perhaps the best way to arrive, however, is by canal, the route of which swings up through the Avon Valley and sweeps majestically into the heart of the built-up area.

THE NATURAL LANDSCAPE

The landscape in this section is dominated by the Avon Valley which carves a path along the eastern edge before falling dramatically into the city of Bath itself. There are a number of excellent vantage points for viewing the valley, with stops along the A36 offering particularly good opportunities. To the west the landscape rises and peaks on the downs of Claverton and Combe, with a golf course prominent south of Bathampton. Two smaller streams, Lam Brook and Catherine's Brook, feature to the north, running into the Avon, while Midford Brook does the same job to the south.

ACCESS AND TRANSPORT

ROADS
The A36 joins the towpath from the south shortly after Avoncliff and sticks with its southern edge up through the Avon valley, passing through Bathampton and Bathwick before linking up with the A4 to the heart of Bath. The A4 itself makes only a brief re-acquaintance with the canal north of Bathampton before heading east. The A46 spurs off the A4 to the north, and the A363 heads south off the same road outside Batheaston on the opposite side of the valley from the A36.

Otherwise, Bath is the natural focus of local trunk roads, with the A367 heading south from the city and the A3062 providing a loop off it to the east via Combe Down. A good network of local roads links the other villages in the section together and provides connections with the trunk roads.

RAIL
The only railway station in this section is Bath Spa, once notable as an important stop on God's Wonderful Railway (or Great Western Railway), but these days run by First Great Western (0845 600 5604). The station is conveniently located in the centre of the city and serves London, South Wales and the West Country.

For more detailed information contact National Train Enquiries on 08457 484950 or www.nationalrail.co.uk.

BUSES
The following list sets out the main bus services on this section although it is advisable to check before using them as some buses only run on certain days and others may have been withdrawn since publication of this Guide. It is also worth checking for more local services, especially those serving Bath and its environs.

- 2 – *Combe Down to Bath (Badgerline)*
- 4 – *Combe Down to Bathampton (Badgerline)*
- 94 – *Trowbridge to Bath via Limpley Stoke and Monkton Combe (Badgerline)*
- 231/232 – *Bath to Chippenham via Batheaston (Badgerline)*
- 265 – *Limpley Stoke to Bath via Claverton and Bathampton (Pickford)*

In addition, the X4 express service takes in Bathampton and Limpley Stoke on its way from Bath to Salisbury, as does the X5 from Bath to Trowbridge/ Warminster, with this latter service also taking in Claverton. Badgerline is based in Weston super Mare (08456 064446) and Pickford in Chippenham (01249 444444).

Traveline (www.traveline.org. uk) on 0870 6082608 can give details of specific services, particularly in Bath, between 7 a.m. and 10 p.m.

Bath Deep Lock.

TAXIS
The following list gives a selection of the taxi operators in this section:

- Absolute Care Mobility Taxis, Bath (01225 404088)
- A1 Taxis, Bath (01225 444777)
- Abbey Taxis, Bath (01225 444444)
- Bath Taxis, Bath (01225 447777)
- Bath Crystal Cars, Bath (01225 482249)
- DC Travel, Bath (01225 401346)
- DCS Cars, Bath (07747 633234)
- Station Taxis, Bath (01225 425678)

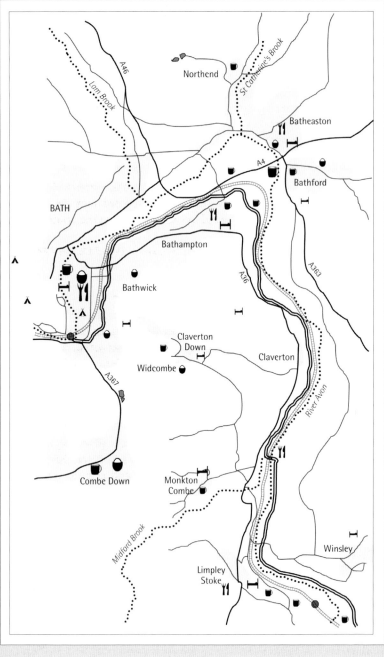

Northend

St Catherine's Brook

A46

Lam Brook

Batheaston

A4

Bathford

BATH

Bathampton

A36

A363

Bathwick

River Avon

A367

Claverton Down

Claverton

Widcombe

Combe Down

Monkton Combe

Midford Brook

Winsley

Limpley Stoke

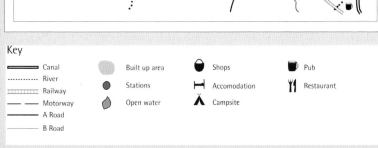

Key

Canal		Built up area		Shops		Pub
River		Stations		Accomodation		Restaurant
Railway		Open water		Campsite		
Motorway						
A Road						
B Road						

BASICS

INTRODUCTION

This whole section seems to be leading up to the splendour that is Bath and as such it is understandable that most shops and places to stay and eat congregate there. The visitor is unlikely to be disappointed, with Bath being many people's favourite city, performing the delicate balancing act of being both a day tripper's tourist destination and a locals' centre with aplomb.

That is not to say that other destinations along this stretch should be ignored in anticipation of Bath, although their contribution lies more in adding variety to the pubs and places to stay than in the retail opportunities they may offer.

Bath also has a major hospital based in Coombe Down (01225 428331).

SHOPPING

Bath acts as a major regional shopping centre and as such it is not surprising that most of the surrounding villages have at best a small selection of local-only stores. There is a small parade of shops at Combe Down with a Co-op, pharmacy and post office, as well as a Tesco Express on the junction with the main road, where there is another small parade. Combe Down also has a branch of Barclays Bank.

On the run in to Bath, Bathford has little to offer shoppers whilst Batheaston has a newsagent, antiques shop, pharmacy and off-licence. Bathampton has a post office, newsagent, hairdresser and pharmacy whilst Widcombe has a run of shops including a health-food shop and a small convenience store within striking distance of the bottom of Bath Locks. Bathwick, meanwhile, has a store with an off-licence.

> Jolly's in Milsom Street (House of Fraser) has claims to be the world's oldest department store and is difficult to miss with its granite, bronze and mahogany shop front.

And so to Bath. Half the city's shops are independently owned, which means it is worth spending time browsing before you buy – you never know what might lie behind the next corner. The city's layout means that there is a preponderance of wide streets, many of them lined with shops, along with a number of small linking passages and alleyways, which are just as likely to turn up something surprising. The big familiar names tend to cluster around the Southgate area, along Stall Street and Union Street as well as the Podium Centre and Milsom Street.

Examples of smaller streets to look out for include Northumberland Place and The Corridor, whilst it is also worth heading out along Walcot Street to the north. Bath is also good for fresh food shops including the Sausage Shop on Green Street, a cheese shop in Quiet Street and another, the Fine Cheese Co., on Walcot Street, as well as numerous bakers and fishmongers. There is also a Farmer's Market every first and third Saturday at Green Park Station. Finally, Bath lives up to its elegant reputation with fashion, hats and shoes being a speciality.

EATING AND DRINKING

As a major tourist destination and university city, Bath offers a good selection of pubs. The following list provides only a sample of what is available, including those on or near the canal or close by the Avon:

- Appleton's, Newbridge (01225 482584)
- The Boater, Argyle Street (01225 464211)
- Boathouse, Newbridge Road (01225 482584)
- Chequers Inn, Rivers Street (01225 424246)
- Curfew Inn, Cleveland Place West (01225 424210)
- Dolphin Inn, Locksbrook Road (01225 445048)
- New Inn, Monmouth Place (01225 332643)
- Old Green Tree, Green Street (01225 448259)
- The Porter, George Street (01225 424104) – *vegetarian pub*
- The Pulteney Arms, Daniel Street (01225 463923)

Otherwise, pubs in other villages and districts along this stretch include:

- The Seven Stars, Winsley (01225 722204)
- Hop Pole Inn, Limpley Stoke (01225 723134)
- Rose and Crown, Limpley Stoke (01225 722237)
- Wheelwrights Arms, Monkton Combe (01225 722287)
- King William IV, Combe Down (01225 833137)
- Foresters Arms, Combe Down (01225 837671)
- Hadley Arms, Combe Down (01225 837117)
- The Horseshoe, Combe Down (01225 837114)
- The Ram, Widcombe (01225 421938)
- The White Hart, Widcombe (01225 313985)
- The Crown, Bathford (01225 852297)
- The George and Dragon, Batheaston (01225 858007)
- The Wagon and Horses, outside Batheaston (01225 858707)
- The Waterwheel, Batheaston (01225 858476) – *pub and restaurant*
- The White Hart, Batheaston (01225 858669)
- The White Lion, Batheaston (01225 858018)
- Northend Inn, Northend (01225 858329)
- Bathampton Mill, Bathampton (01225 469758) – *pub and restaurant*
- The George, Bathampton (01225 425079) – *on the canal*

Inevitably, there is a wealth of choice when it comes to eating in Bath. The following list provides just a sample of what is available:

- Bathtub Bistro, Grove Street (01225 460593) – *bistro with good vegetarian selection*
- Café Retro, York Street (01225 339347) – *popular café and restaurant*
- Demuth's, North Parade Passage (01225 446059) – *vegetarian*
- Eastern Eye, Quiet Street (01225 422323) – *Indian*
- Fishworks, Green Street (01225 488707) – *seafood*
- Hole in the Wall, George Street (01225 425242) – *Michelin grade food*
- Mai Thai, Pierrepont Street (01225 445557) – *Thai*
- The Moon and Sixpence, Broad Street (01225 460962) – *International*
- No. 5, Argyle Street (01225 444499) – *French*
- Olive Tree, Russel Street (01225 447928) – *Mediterranean*
- Popjoys, Beau Nash House (01225 460494) – *traditional*
- Rajpoot, Argyle Street (01225 466833) – *Indian*
- Walrus and the Carpenter, Barton St (01225 314864) – *good for salads*
- Xian, Charles Street (01225 424917) – *Chinese*

It is almost obligatory to try a Bath bun whilst in the city and there is plenty of choice for places that serve them; the most famous is probably Sally Lunns in North Parade Passage (01225 461634). Otherwise there is the Pulteney Bridge Café or the teahouse at the Hulburne Museum (see 'Seeing and Doing').

   Places to eat outside of Bath include the following, although many of the pubs listed opposite also offer food:
- Angelfish Café, Limpley Stoke (01225 723483) – *at the Canal Centre*
- Nightingales Restaurant, Limpley Stoke (01225 723150) – *Italian*
- The Fat Friar, Fish and Chips in Batheaston (01225 852467)
- The Waterwheel, Batheaston (01225 858476) – *pub and restaurant*
- Bathampton Mill, Bathampton (01225 469758) – *pub and restaurant*

SLEEPING

Bath's status means its honey stone makes it something of a honey pot when it comes to places to stay, with all depths of pocket catered for.

HOTELS IN BATH

If you feel like treating yourself, options include the following:

- Abbey Hotel (01225 461603) – *centrally located in North Parade*
- The Ayrlington (01225 425495) – *Victorian house in its own gardens with private parking*
- Bath Spa Hotel (0870 400 8222) – *Spa hotel in a Georgian mansion*
- The County Hotel (01225 425003) – *close to centre with own car park*

- Pratt's Hotel (01225 460441)
  – *quiet and friendly*
- The Queensbury Hotel
  (01225 447928) – *four Georgian houses in a quiet street with the*
- *Olive Tree Restaurant attached*
- The Royal Crescent Hotel
  (01225 823333) – *exclusive hotel in the Royal Crescent*

More mid-ranged hotels in the city include:

- Brompton House
  (01225 420972)
- Carfax Hotel (01225 462089)
  The Francis on the Square
  (0870 400 8223)
- Harington's Hotel
  (01225 461728)
- Haydon House (01225 444919)
  – *Edwardian town house*
- Kennard Hotel (01225 310472)
  – *Georgian town house*

- Lodge Hotel (01225 858373)
- Pulteney House Hotel (01225 460991) – *Victorian town house*
- The Royal Hotel (01225 463134) – *by the railway station*
- Sydney Gardens Hotel
  (01225 464818)
- Tasburgh House Hotel
  (01225 425096) – *Victorian mansion with gardens alongside the canal*

HOTELS OUTSIDE BATH

- Homewood Park Hotel and Restaurant, outside Limpley Stoke (01225 723731)
- The Cliffe Hotel, Limpley Stoke (01225 723226) – *family-run hotel with just 11 rooms*
- Holiday Inn Express
  (0870 444 2792) – *modern hotel 1 mile from centre*
- The Limpley Stoke Hotel, Limpley Stoke (01225 723333) – *Georgian country house hotel*
- The Waterside Hotel, Widcombe (01225 338855) – *modern hotel on the Widcombe Basin*
- Avondale Hotel and Restaurant,

  Batheaston (01225 859847)
- Bailbrook Lodge Hotel, Bathford (01225 859090)
- The Old Mill Hotel, Batheaston (01225 858476)
- Combe Grove Manor Hotel, Monkton Combe (01225 834644) – *eighteenth-century manor near to the canal*
- Monkshill, Monkton Combe (01225 833028)
- The Manor House, Monkton Combe (0845 3453972) – *medieval manor*
- Ravenscroft, Bathwick (01225 461919)

BED AND BREAKFAST/GUEST HOUSES

Less expensive accommodation in Bath includes:

- Avon Guest House
  (01225 313009)
- Brinsley Sheridan House
  (01225 429562)

- Lynwood House (01225 426410)
- Membland Guest House
  (01225 599572)
- Milton House (01225 335632)

- The Old Red Lion
  (01225 330464)
- Radnor Guest House

Others further afield include:

- Serendipity B&B, Winsley
  (01225 722380)
- Stillmeadow, Winsley
  (01225 722119)
- Millbrook, Limpley Stoke
  (01225 723818)
- Monkshill Guest House, Monkton
  Combe (01225 833028)
- Wheelwrights Arms, Monkton
  Combe (01225 722287) – *8 rooms
  based in a pub*
- Mendip View, Combe Down
  (01225 835897)
- Rainbow Wood Farm B&B,
  towards Claverton Down
  (01225 466366)
- Lindesfarne Guest House
  (01225 466342), Bathampton
- Bamboo Gardens B&B,

(01225 316159)
- The White Guest House
  (01225 426075)

Bathampton church.

Batheaston (01225 859922)
- Dolphin House, Batheaston
  (01225 858915)
- Greenways, Bathwick
  (01225 310132)

Bath also has a splendid youth hostel based in an Italianate mansion with its own gardens on the Bathwick Road (0870 770 5688).

CAMPING

There are two main camping sites around Bath, both offering extensive facilities:
- Bath Marina and Caravan Park (01225 424301)
- Newton Mill Caravan and Camping (01225 333909) – *90 hard standing and over 100 tent pitches with free fishing and woodland walking*

Bath is also the place to go for camping and walking equipment, with no less than six shops to choose from.
   The nearest camping supplies outlets in this section are:
- BCH Camping and Leisure, Southgate, Bath (01225 460200)
- Itchy Feet, Bartlett Street, Bath (020 7292 9750)
- Oswald Bailey, Southgate, Bath (01225 463202)
- Blacks, High Street, Bath (01225 471500)
- Millets, Southgate, Bath (01225 429596)
- Explore, Upper Borough Walls, Bath (01225 463833)

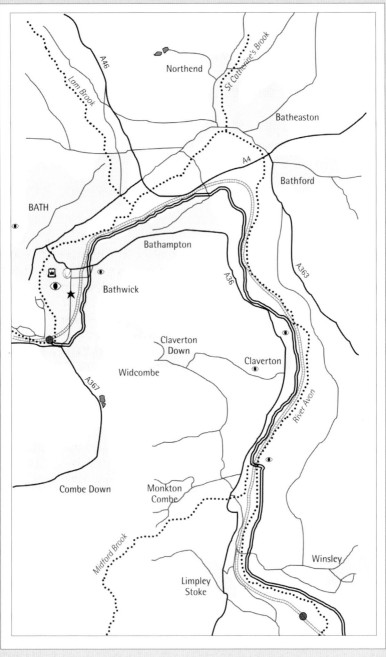

Northend

St Catherine's Brook

A46

Lam Brook

Batheaston

Bathford

BATH

A4

Bathampton

Bathwick

A363

A36

Claverton Down

Claverton

Widcombe

River Avon

A367

Monkton Combe

Combe Down

Midford Brook

Winsley

Limpley Stoke

Key

▬▬ Canal		⬭ Built up area	◉ Site/Sight
⋯⋯ River		⬮ Stations	◌ Leisure
▥▥ Railway		⬯ Open water	★ Entertainment
▬ ▬ Motorway			⬛ Culture
▬▬ A Road			
▬ B Road			

SEEING AND DOING

INTRODUCTION

Although Bath acts as a natural magnet for visitors to this area, with some justification as there is much to see there, it would be a shame to miss out on some of the attractions leading up to the city, both manmade and natural. The Limpley Stoke Valley overlooking the Avon in particular is a sight for sore eyes and there are a number of good vantage points along the A36.

SIGHTS

This section starts spectacularly with Brassknocker Basin and its canal centre at the end of a remnant of the old Somerset Coal Canal. There is a restaurant and bike centre here as well as a room with exhibits covering the immediate area, which gives background on not only the two canals but also the Somerset and Dorset Railway. It is also possible to hire self-drive day boats here (electricity powered) as well as canoes (01225 722292).

> Boaters should be aware that it is only possible to turn boats up to 60ft at Brassknocker Basin and that they should check beforehand that even this will be possible as it can get crowded.

Wander down the arm for a few hundred yards and you come to the spectacular Dundas Aqueduct. From here it is possible to appreciate your position in the heart of the Limpley Stoke Valley, with great views either side of the Aqueduct, which it is possible to walk along. The structure itself is worth pausing to consider and underwent considerable restoration in order to reopen the canal. Built by John Rennie, it is shorter than the nearby Avoncliff but offers more dramatic views.

> The Somerset & Dorset Railway was also known as the 'slow and dirty' line. A Beeching victim, the line is probably best remembered for its Pines Express which brought passengers from the Midlands to Weymouth for their summer holidays.

Further down the canal lies the Claverton Pumping Station (01225 483001), another Rennie building. This is normally open every Sunday, Wednesday and Bank Holiday between Easter and October and was built to raise water up from the Avon to the canal using a waterwheel-powered beam engine. The pump was necessary to replace water lost by the Bath Locks and dates back to the early nineteenth century.

Before leaving this area it is worth considering the American Museum at Claverton (01225 460503) which looks at aspects of the American way of life from Colonial times to the eve of the Civil War. A particular feature is the replica of George Washington's Mount Vernon Garden and a Colonial herb garden, from where it is possible to absorb some more spectacular views out over the valley.

Bathwick, just before the city, is worth passing through even if you do not decide to stop as it has some curious architecture on display and is the location of the technical end of the Kennet & Avon Canal before it becomes the River Avon. It is also the home of the Holburne Museum (01225 466669) which houses the collection of Sir William Holburne. This extends across silver and old master paintings as well as Italian bronzes, glass, furniture, porcelain and portrait miniatures.

As a tourist destination Bath is lucky to have at least two pools of interest to draw on when presenting itself to its public. First there are the Roman Baths, and then there is the legacy of its period in the sun as the Regency 'place to be'. The first of these is perhaps the best-known internationally, with the Baths (01225 477785) open to the public all year round, offering an impressive sight.

It is possible to take guided tours round the baths but the audio guides make a good job of taking you round. You can still see the water still rising and the sight of one of the baths bubbling away is always worth a repeat viewing. Finally, there are the Pump Rooms where you can sample the water and then have a cup of tea in magnificent surroundings to take the disgusting taste away!

Plenty of tangible evidence of the Regency heyday also remains, not least the impressive Royal Crescent and the Circus, as well as the Assembly Rooms (01225 477785), which also house the Museum of Costume. There is also a museum dedicated to explaining how Bath ended up looking the way it does (The Building of Bath Museum 01225 333895). Finally, do not forget (as

> Caroline Hershel was the first woman to be elected to the Royal Society and was responsible for discovering no less than eight new comets.

if you could miss it) Pulteney Bridge, one of only three shop-lined bridges in the world.

Other museums worth thinking about include the Postal Museum (01225 460333), the Jane Austen Centre (01225 443000), both of which are self-explanatory, No.1 Royal Crescent (01225 428126) which shows what one of the houses on the Crescent would have looked like in the eighteenth century, and William Herschel House (01225 311342) celebrating the work of the astronomer and his sister Caroline.

Being a city also means that Bath has its own cathedral or Abbey, known as the 'Lantern of the West' because of the light that

> The Royal Victoria Park is the venue of Bath's famous Balloon Festival when hot air balloons of every conceivable shape take to the air.

floods through its windows. The Abbey also has the Heritage Vaults (01225 422462) which explore the history of religious buildings on this site.

Slightly out of town, there is the Beckford Tower and Museum (01225 422212), a folly built by William Beckford filled with furniture and art and crowned with a magnificent lantern. The tower sits at the end of a mill, a long landscaped ride that leads to the top of Lansdown Hill.

Bath is also known for its gardens, which include the Parade Gardens right in the centre by the river and close to Pulteney Bridge, Sydney Gardens (said to be Jane Austen's favourite), and Royal Victoria Park amongst others. The latter includes a Botanical Garden as well as a children's park and crazy golf course.

This is only a sample of what is available in Bath, which needs more than a day to do it justice. If time is not on your side a visit to the Tourist Information Centre in the Abbey Chambers (01225 477101) should be your first stop, or alternatively one of the open-top bus tours represent a good option (Bath Bus Co. 01225 330444, City Sightseeing 01708 866000).

CULTURE AND ENTERTAINMENT

Bath offers much in the way of cultural stimulation with the Theatre Royal in Sawclose the main venue (01225 448844). Other venues include the Assembly Rooms and the Abbey, whilst the city runs an annual Mozartfest every November (01225 429750). Other festivals include the International Music Festival held during the last two weeks in May of each year and the Literature Festival held in early March (01225 463362).

Bath has two cinemas, the recently opened Odeon at the Kingsmead Leisure Centre (0871 2244007), and the Little Theatre (01225 466822), an art-house cinema. For those looking to get a little more active there is the Bath Sports and Leisure Centre on North Parade Road (01225 462565) which boasts a gym, swimming pool and sports hall.

If you are looking to take advantage of the river you can do worse than head for the Bath Boating Station on Forester Road (01225 466407), a Victorian boating station which offers punts, skiffs and canoes for hire and is also a good spot to look for waterlife, possibly from the comfort of the tea garden. Alternatively, you can take a powered boat trip up to Pulteney Weir and pretend you are approaching Niagara Falls (01225 480541).

As night falls there is the option of taking one of the acclaimed 'Bizarre Bath' walks, described as being 'hysterical not historical', in which actors take you for a walk around the city and interpret some of the events that have helped shape it. These run every night from 8 p.m. (01225 335124).

No doubt aided by the large student population, Bath is well served with nightclubs, with the main ones being:
• Babylon, Kingston Road (01225 465002)
• Cadillacs, Walcot Street (01225 464241)
• The Common Room, Saville Row (01225 425550)
• Moles, George Street (01225 404446)
• Po Na Na, North Parade (01225 401115)

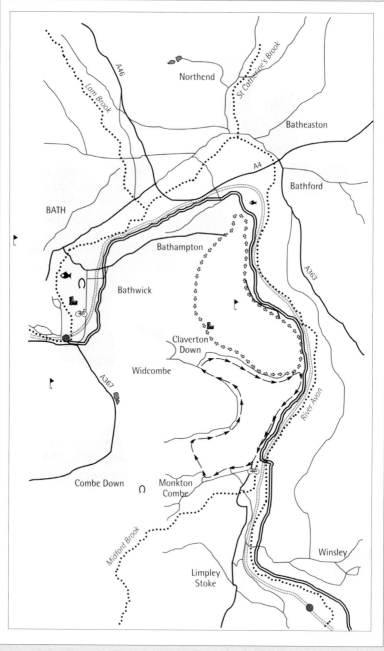

Key

Canal	Built up area	Cycling route/outlet	Riding outlet
River	Stations	Walking route/outlet	Golf course/outlet
Railway	Open water	Fishing spot/outlet	
Motorway			
A Road			
B Road			

Northend

A46

Lam Brook

St Catherine's Brook

Batheaston

A4

Bathford

BATH

Bathampton

A363

Bathwick

Claverton Down

Widcombe

River Avon

A367

Combe Down

Monkton Combe

Midford Brook

Limpley Stoke

Winsley

SAMPLING

INTRODUCTION

The Avon Valley dominates this stretch which offers a number of sampling opportunities, be they on water, foot or wheel. The downs to the south of Bath offer wonderful views, including those from a circular walk, as do the western sides of the valley itself. The Bathampton Mill pub in Bathampton itself offers a separate section of its car park for those looking to leave their cars and explore the local area.

> Day boat hire is possible from both the Canal Centre at Limpley Stoke (www.bath-narrowboats-trips.co.uk) on MV *Jubilee* (01749 850169) and from the Avondale Hotel in Batheaston (01225 859847).

The OS Explorer Map covering this stretch is No.155, Bristol and Bath.

WALKING

The main designated path through this section is the Limestone Link which passes through Limpley Stoke and Batheaston. This 36-mile path links the Cotswolds to the Mendips, hence its name. The Avon walkway also passes through Bath.

> Built in 1810 by John Rennie to replace the water lost at the Bath Locks, the Claverton Pumping Station could raise 100,000 gallons from the Avon.

Bushey Norwood, just south of Bath, was planted in the nineteenth century to provide parkland on the edge of Bath and is now maintained by the National Trust. Look out here for tree-creepers, nut hatches and green woodpeckers as well as cowslips and early purple orchids in the spring. These days this is part of the wider Bath Skyline trail, a 6-mile circular walk with its own map available from the National Trust website.

Walk F passes to the south and east of Bath and affords some excellent views across to the city, as well as an opportunity to visit both the Avon and Claverton Pumping Station.

SECTION F WALK
To Bathhampton via Claverton

Description:	*Some steep gradients either side of the canal, with a golf course and woods straddling the top of the valley.*
Distance:	*4½ miles*
Duration:	*1½hrs*
Staring point:	*Grid Reference 788641, OS Explorer 155*
Nearest refreshment:	*Pubs in Bathampton*

Start in Claverton, taking the footpath opposite the church and across the road down to the canal. Just before Bridge 180 divert to the right if you wish to visit Claverton Pumping Station. For the walk continue along the towpath to Bridge 182, Bathampton Swing Bridge. Cross over the bridge and follow the path uphill to the left, down a track and past some houses in Bathampton.

At a T-junction turn left, cross over the A36 and follow the bridleway opposite uphill. Bear left at a Y-junction and on reaching a fence take a right, emerging out onto some open land with magnificent views. Bear left and pass through a gate and continue with the path, turning left again at an enclosed reservoir. Head out right across the golf course and left at a gate, following the edge of a wood. On entering the wood bear right and then turn right into Bushey Norwood, following its left-hand edge.

On reaching fresh woods bear right and on exiting the trees turn left and then left again on reaching the road. Follow this downhill back to Claverton, passing the American Museum on the way.

Walking equipment outlets along this section include:
- BCH Camping and Leisure, Bath (01225 460200)
- Blacks, Bath (01225 471500)
- Explore, Bath (01225 463833)
- Itchy Feet, Bath (01225 460046)
- Millets, Bath (01225 429596)

CYCLING

National Cycle Routes 4 and 24 meet at Brassknocker Basin, with the former going north into Bath and south towards Claverton and beyond, whilst the latter takes in Monkton Combe and Bradford on Avon. This remains a good place to cycle, with a good variety of vehicles also available for hire at Brassknocker Basin (01225 722292) as well as in Bath, notably Avon Valley Cyclery at the back of the railway station (01225 461880).

To sample this section on two wheels start at the Brassknocker Basin and head west towards Monkton Combe on Route 24. On reaching the village head north and then north-west, following roads until you reach a T-junction where you turn right. Follow this road as it sweeps around the southern limit of Claverton Down and heads north.

On reaching a junction with a minor road just before the village of Claverton Down head right and then downhill into Claverton. Turn north briefly on the A36, picking up the footpath on the right down to the pumping station. On finding the towpath head right (south) and follow this back to the junction with the Somerset Coal Canal, taking the path south of the Canal back to the basin. All told this ride represents just over 7 miles, but may seem more given the gradients involved.

Cycle outlets along this section include:

- Hare's Cycles, Moorland Road, Bath (01225 422674)
- John's Bikes, Walcot Street, Bath (01225 334633)
- Total Fitness, Saracen Street, Bath (01225 444164)

RIDING

Riders are not particularly well served along this stretch. Other than the towpath there is some bridleway between Bathampton and Claverton and north-east out of Bathford, with the local roads not particularly horse-friendly either.

Horse-riding establishments and outlets along this section include:
- Midford Valley Riding Centre, Midford, Bath (01225 837613)
- Totally Tack, Bath (01373 834987)
- Wellow Trekking Centre, Bath (0125 834376)
- Weston Farm, Weston, Bath (01225 483483)

FISHING

Canal fishing throughout this stretch is controlled by the Bathampton AA (01225 338127) where it is possible to catch roach (around 2lb), bream (up to 5lb), tench (up to 3lb), perch and gudgeon. There are also chub around Claverton rising up to 20lb, as well as some smaller pike. The Association also controls waters on the River Avon alongside the canal, notably at Claverton where there is the Long Meadow with large roach, chub and bream; The Island for barbell, chub and pike; and The Manor Field, for pike, chub, roach, bream, perch and barbell.

Bath is also home to Cycle Rides Ltd, organisers of the annual London to Brighton Bike ride amongst other charitable events.

In addition, the Association offers part of the Avon at Batheaston off a triangular piece of land on right-hand bank downstream of the Toll Bridge opposite the weir. Although there are only three swims, the potential is enormous. Look out for good barbell and pike.

Outlets selling fishing supplies along this stretch include:
- Bacon's Tackle Box, Lower Bristol Road, Bath (01225 448850)
- Orvis Company Store Shop, Pulteney Bridge (01225 331471)

OTHER

Golfers are fairly well catered for in this area, with an 18-hole course on the downs overlooking the city, another to the north and two municipal courses:

Bath Golf Club is the sixth oldest in the country and was opened at the end of 1879.

- Bath Approach Golf Course, Weston Road (01225 331162)
  – *two par-3 courses in Victoria*

Park with great views over Bath

• Bath Golf Club (01225 463834) – 18 holes, 6,442 yards, a mile south-east of the city on the A36, again with great views

• Entry Hill Golf Course, Entry Hill (01225 834248) – 9-hole course

Brassknocker Basin, Limpley Stoke.

LEARN MORE AND LINKS

For those wishing to delve a little further into the places and events covered in this guide, the following list, whilst far from comprehensive, should act as a useful starting point:

TOURIST INFORMATION
www.katrust.org – Kennet & Avon Trust website
Bath (0906 7112000)
Bradford on Avon (01225 865797)
Devizes TIC (01380 729408)
Melksham (01225 707424)
Newbury (01635 30267)
Pewsey Information Point (01672 564364)
Reading (0118 956 6226)
Trowbridge (01225 710535)

WEBSITES OFFERING INFORMATION ON SPECIFIC PLACES OR EVENTS:
www.berkshirehistory.com – good for snapshots of the history of Berkshire towns and villages
www.reading.gov.uk – website for Reading Borough Council
www.clicknewbury.com – general Newbury site
www.greenham-common.org.uk – guides to Greenham and Crookham Commons
www.newburynow.com – d
irectory of Newbury businesses
www.newburytowncentre.co.uk/ – another Newbury site
www.visitwiltshire.co.uk – tourism site for Wiltshire
www.wiltshire-web.co.uk/history – Wiltshire history
www.wiltshire.gov.uk/community – Wiltshire history
www.pewsey.co.uk – Pewsey local website
www.burbage-wiltshire.co.uk – Burbage information
www.devizes.co.uk – Devizes information
www.avoncliff.co.uk – Avoncliff information
www.monktoncombe.com – Monkton Combe information
www.batheaston.net – Batheaston and Northend information
www.bathampton-village.org.uk – Bathampton information
www.visitbath.co.uk – Bath information
www.cityofbath.co.uk – more Bath information

FISHING
www.amberarc.co.uk/angling/bathampton – Bathampton AA
www.devizesaa.org.uk – Devizes AA
www.csasonline.com – Civil Service AA
www.rdaa.co.uk – Reading and District AA
www.thatchamaa.co.uk – Thatcham AA

LOCALLY PRODUCED FOOD
www.bigbarn.co.uk – the UK's main site for locally produced food

CROP CIRCLES
www.cropcircleconnector.com

BOOKS OFFERING FURTHER DETAIL ON SPECIFIC PLACES OR ASPECTS OF LOCAL HISTORY:

The Kennet & Avon Canal, Helen Hackford, Clive Hackford (Tempus Publishing 2001)

The Wiltshire & Berkshire Canal, Doug Small (Tempus Publishing 2001)

Pub Walks Along the Kennet and Avon Canal, Nigel Vine (Countryside Books 1997)

The Kennet and Avon Canal, John Russell (Millstream Books 1997)

Restoring the Kennet & Avon Canal, Peter Lindley Jones (Tempus Publishing 2002)

The Kennet and Avon Canal: A Journey from Newbury to Bath in 1964, John Russell (Millstream Books 1997)

TRANSPORT
www.readingcyclingcampaign.org.uk – details on cycling routes in Reading.
www.readingctc.co.uk – website for Reading CTC.
Sustrans Information Service, PO Box 21, Bristol BS99 2HA (0117 929 0888) www.sustrans.org.uk
Traveline (www.traveline.org.uk) on 0870 6082608 for train routes and times

OTHER
www.nationaltrust.org.uk – website for the National Trust, useful in particular for more on the properties mentioned in the Guide.
www.ramblers.org.uk
The British Horse Society, Stoneleigh Deer Park, Kenilworth, Warks CV8 2XZ (08701 202244).

Bathampton Swing Bridge.

INDEX

Tempus is keen to keep these guides as up to date as possible. If you have any suggestions for inclusion in the next edition of this guide, or would like to point out any changes since it was written, please email us at towpathguides@tempus-publishing.com

If you are interested in purchasing other books published by Tempus, or in case you have difficulty finding any Tempus books in your local bookshop, you can also place orders directly through our website

www.tempus-publishing.com